# THE 39TH BIENNIAL EXHIBITION OF CONTEMPORARY AMERICAN PAINTING

THE CORCORAN GALLERY OF ART
Washington, D.C.
February 2–April 7, 1985

THE MARY AND LEIGH BLOCK GALLERY
Northwestern University
Evanston, Illinois
April 26–July 7, 1985

THE BUTLER INSTITUTE OF AMERICAN ART
Youngstown, Ohio
September 8–October 13, 1985

CONTEMPORARY ARTS CENTER
Cincinnati, Ohio
October 24–November 30, 1985

This exhibition and catalogue have been made possible by grants from the Anna E. Clark Fund and the National Endowment for the Arts.

In 1927, Anna E. Clark, the widow of Senator William A. Clark, established a fund for the perpetuation of the Biennial.

# THE 39TH BIENNIAL EXHIBITION OF CONTEMPORARY AMERICAN PAINTING

Lisa Lyons

THE CORCORAN GALLERY OF ART
WASHINGTON, D.C.

Library of Congress ISSN 8756-4777
ISBN 0-88675-015-6

Edited by Nancy Eickel

Designed by Alex and Caroline Castro, Hollowpress, Baltimore

Printed by Schneidereith and Sons, Baltimore

# TABLE OF CONTENTS

## Lenders to the Exhibition

Paul A. Anderson
Daniel and Daisy Belin
Charles B. Benenson
Robert H. Bergman
Steven Berkowitz
Bruce and Lois Berry
Toni Birckhead Gallery, Cincinnati
Macyn Bolt
Peder Bonnier
Dr. Mary Jo Brandt
John Broenen
James I.W. Corcoran
Dart Gallery, Chicago
Stefan T. Edlis/Neeson Collection
Feature, Chicago
First Bank Minneapolis
James P. Gardiner
Getler/Pall/Saper Gallery, New York
Barbara Gladstone Gallery, New York
Erwin B. and Barbara Glass
Marc and Phyllis Goldish
Emily and Roger Hill
Mark Jackson and Ken Hodorowski
Lance Kiland
Phyllis Kind Gallery, New York and Chicago
Patrick King
Patrick King Contemporary Art, Indianapolis
Sherry and Alan Koppel
J. Jeffry Kotler
Rose and Morton Landowne
Mr. and Mrs. Robert C. Larson
Dr. Robert Lebow
Robert Lehrman
Corrine and Leonard Lemberg
Patricia Locke
Robert Lostutter
Memphis Brooks Museum of Art
The Metropolitan Museum of Art
Kay Miller
Peter Miller Gallery, Chicago
Museum of Art, Rhode Island School of Design
Michael Nakoneczny
Walter and Dawn Clark Netsch
Ken Nevadomi
Osuna Gallery, Washington, D.C.
Fredrik Roos
Laila and Thurston Twigg-Smith
Dorothy Sahn
Dr. and Mrs. Jorge Schneider
Dorothy Schramm
Hollis Sigler
Martin Sklar
Dr. and Mrs. Steven Valfer
James Varchmin Gallery/Lonn Frye, Chicago
Laura-Lee Woods
One Private Collection

# PREFACE

The prospect of organizing and presenting an exhibition that hopes to convey some sense of what is going on in American painting in the previous two years is a daunting one, but the Corcoran has taken this task on 38 times before. It was certainly easier in 1907 when America and American painting was more defined and definable. Today the task is infinitely more complex.

This exhibition became a reality because of the enthusiastic support and commitment of the artists. They made key examples of their work available for this presentation and submitted to lengthy interviews during which they supplied important information about their methods and subjects. We are also indebted to the many private collectors and institutional lenders listed elsewhere in this catalogue who generously parted with their treasured works so these paintings could be appreciated by a wide audience.

Thanks also go to the following dealers and their staffs who supplied critical literature and photographic materials, made major works available for the exhibition, and provided valuable assistance in securing several loans: Toni Birckhead, Toni Birckhead Gallery, Cincinnati; Rebecca Blattberg, André Stone, Melissa Bernens, and Victoria Espy, Dart Gallery, Chicago; Hudson, Feature, Chicago; Helen Getler, Carol Saper, and Susan Putterman, Getler/Pall/Saper Gallery, New York; Phyllis Kind and William H. Bengtson, Phyllis Kind Gallery, Chicago and New York; Chris Middendorf, Middendorf Gallery, Washington, D.C.; Ramon Osuna, Osuna Gallery, Washington, D.C.; Holly and Horace Solomon, Cee Brown, Anita Grossman, and Esther Schwartz, Holly Solomon Gallery, New York; William vanStraaten and Kathy Cottong, vanStraaten Gallery, Inc., Chicago; and Roberta Lieberman, Robert Zolla, and Judith Simon, Zolla/Lieberman Gallery, Chicago.

In the planning stages of this exhibition, numerous colleagues were helpful in directing us to the work of talented artists throughout the Midwest. For their advice and counsel, we are particularly grateful to Russell Bowman, Jane Brite, James Demetrion, Jane Farver, Helen Ferrulli, Thomas Garver, Marge Goldwater, Tom Hinson, Robert Hobbs, Mary Jane Jacob, Lance Kinz, Sarah Rogers-Lafferty, Robert Murdock, Trent Myers, William Olander, Anne Rorimer, Sandra Wilcoxon, and Martha Winans.

The key to the success of this enterprise is of course Lisa Lyons. She has indefatigably worked the studios, the curators, the collectors, the museums and the dealers. She has rolled up impressive mileage, but more impressive is the depth of the sampling her work provided. She has seen an enormous amount of work and has gone about the very difficult task of shaping it into a cogent exhibition with clarity.

We would like to thank Martha Williams for typing Lisa Lyons' catalogue manuscript and acknowledge the support of Richard Grossman, Gwen Bitz, Mark Blackman, John Friday, and Henry Geyelin. Cathy Card Sterling oversaw the myriad of details that are inevitable in an exhibition of this scope, and Elizabeth D. Beam expertly coordinated the complex movement of the paintings from so many places. Nancy Eickel was invaluable in assisting with the preparation of this catalogue.

We are also grateful to our colleagues, Kathy Kelsy Foley, Director, Mary and Leigh Block Gallery, Evanston, Illinois; Mr. Louis Zona, Director, The Butler Institute of American Art, Youngstown, Ohio; and Dennis Barrie, Director, Contemporary Arts Center, Cincinnati, Ohio, for helping to make the tour of the exhibition a success.

Michael Botwinick
Director

# INTRODUCTION

*The 39th Biennial Exhibition of Contemporary American Painting* is conceived as the second in a series of Corcoran Biennials which deal successively with large regions of the United States. The history of this venerable Corcoran tradition—the Biennial may indeed be said to be an institution in American art—dates back to the beginning of this century and represents a number of evolutionary manifestations. From an enormous national invitational show, to a "juried" exhibition, to a number of events which truly reflected the incredible innovations of the 1960s and '70s, to a recent series of rigorously limited exhibitions focusing on new works by our greatest living masters, this ongoing show of recent American painting reflects its times in extraordinarily sensitive ways.

The diversity and richness of painting in the United States in this period of our history makes it virtually impossible to do justice to the entire range of good work in a single exhibition. Thus, we are concentrating on sections of the country. Two years ago, with the 38th Biennial, we presented works by artists from the Far West and Southwest. This year's exhibition focuses on the Midwestern states of Illinois, Iowa, Indiana, Ohio, Michigan, Minnesota, and Wisconsin. As curator Lisa Lyons in her catalogue text describes the common denominator operating through her selection process, and as the works themselves show us, there is a fascinating unity of concern resonating among the seventeen painters included. More significantly, and more symptomatically of the state of painting throughout America, there is also a tremendous variety of styles and concerns and techniques. It doesn't add up to a "regional style" nor does it truly *deny* the existence of an affinity among contemporaries who happen to live in a particular geographic region.

If, as I think it must, the Corcoran Biennial does truly reflect existing tendencies and changes in the painting of our time, this show reveals a gratifying reality: good painting, fresh and accomplished and inventive work, flourishes in all parts of our country. The slow process of the decentralization of culture which has been underway for the past few decades is reaching a demonstrable maturity.

Jane Livingston
Associate Director and Chief Curator

## THE ARTISTS

Nicholas Africano
Macyn Bolt
John Broenen
Roger Brown
Peter Huttinger
Tom Keesee
Lance Kiland
Robert Lostutter
Jim Lutes
Kay Miller
Michael Nakoneczny
Dennis Nechvatal
Ken Nevadomi
Jim Nutt
Ed Paschke
Hollis Sigler
T.L. Solien

Given the international nature of the current art scene, does the notion of regionalism hold any validity for a discussion of contemporary painting in the United States? Is it any longer meaningful, or even possible, to characterize the art produced in one part of the country in some way that will easily distinguish it from the art of other regions? These were among the questions I pondered when I was invited to organize *The 39th Biennial Exhibition of Contemporary American Painting*, an exhibition devoted to recent painting in seven midwestern states: Illinois, Indiana, Iowa, Michigan, Minnesota, Ohio, and Wisconsin.

Philosophical as well as practical considerations entered into the Corcoran's decision to sponsor a regional exhibition. The curatorial staff recognized that years after numerous pronouncements had been made about its demise, painting was once again alive and well and thriving in the United States. It was felt that several exhibitions would be required to do justice to the newly vital scene. Geography seemed the most logical way to divvy up the embarrassment of riches confronting the museum. Thus, in 1983 the Corcoran inaugurated a series of regional Biennials with an exhibition surveying recent painting in ten western states.

The ground rules for the present exhibition, the second in the series, were few. After agreeing on the territory to be covered, my colleagues at the Corcoran and I discussed the criteria for selection. "Midwesternism," that is, the revelation of a peculiarly regional spirit, was not among them. In fact, we determined that aside from geography, quality would be the sole criterion. Perhaps that sounds vague, but what a marvelous assignment! "Assemble an exhibition of the finest painting now being produced in the Midwest." It seemed a curator's fantasy of a true exercise in connoisseurship.

As the fantasy became reality and I conducted the first of many odysseys through the states, it quickly became apparent that there were a great many talented painters in the region. There were far too many, in fact, to be represented in anything but a mammoth, salon-style exhibition consisting of one work by each artist. I believed that such an exhibition would very likely be unsatisfying, perhaps incomprehensible and, in the final analysis, a disservice to both the artists and the public. I quickly opted for another approach: an exhibition featuring a relatively small number of painters, one that would give the public an opportunity to study the recent production of each artist in some depth. By showing three to five works by each painter, I felt viewers would gain a more meaningful understanding of individual artistic identity.

With that approach in mind, I began to hone my vision and ultimately selected seventeen painters whose work most insistently drew my attention. All these artists share an interest in representational imagery, and several, like many of their contemporaries on the international scene, emphasize the figure in their work.

This exhibition is not intended to be a comprehensive survey but rather a selective look at some of the most accomplished representational work in the region. It is not limited to young and unknown artists. In an attempt to draw a truer picture of the dynamics of the current art scene, it includes individuals of various ages and career stages. Of the seventeen artists whose work is on view, some have already established international reputations; others have only begun recently to show their work nationally; for still others, the Corcoran Biennial represents the first opportunity to exhibit their work in a major museum outside the cities in which they live.

In discussing the territory surveyed in this exhibition, a case could be made for considering it a microcosm of the entire nation. Within the midwestern cultural universe, Chicago occupies a position analogous to that occupied by New York City in the national scene. It is the major art marketplace, home to numerous established artists, collectors, museums, galleries, alternative spaces, and schools of various persuasions and, not suprisingly, a place to which many young artists gravitate. The region boasts several other cultural centers; prominent among them is Minneapolis. Thanks in part to the presence of the Walker Art Center, The Minneapolis Institute of Arts, numerous schools, and theater and dance companies, as well as the existence of bountiful corporate and foundation funding, the city attracts many artists from around the country. Inadequate critical coverage and a limited marketplace aside, Minneapolis offers artists the inviting combination of a quiet atmosphere and a relatively high level of cultural sophistication. Museums, art centers, galleries, and alternative spaces of every description are found in cities throughout the region, including Akron, Cincinnati, Cleveland, Dayton, Oberlin, Toledo, Youngstown, Madison, Milwaukee, Detroit, Grand Rapids, and Indianapolis, to give only a partial listing.[1]

From time to time, artists sharing similar aesthetic aims can be identified with each locale. Chicago, for example, was the birthplace in the mid–1960s of the movement now commonly referred to as Imagism. As Russell Bowman observes in the exhibition catalogue *Who Chicago?*, Imagism no longer exists as a group manifestation. It lives on as a *style* in the number of artists who continue to evolve important work from its assumptions and approaches.[2] Generally speaking, however, hard and fast characterizations of the art produced in Chicago, or in any other city within the region for that matter, are destined to have only the most fleeting currency. As it is often said, ideas generated in one place quickly find echoes and responses in many other locations. As the critic Dennis Adrian has observed, "The wide ranging mobility of contemporary artists, the increasing volume of publications about them, the ever increasing activities of museums, commercial galleries, and art centers of all kinds everywhere have produced a truly global visual culture."[3] The American academic establishment especially has contributed to the development of a scene in flux in this country. Anti-tenure track policies and visiting artist programs have spawned a new generation of itinerant painters—the academic nomads—whose stylistic seeds sprout in quick succession in many cities around the nation.

Of course, the Midwest still is not exactly the center of the art world (although a walk through Chicago's thriving gallery district, nicknamed SuHu, tempts one to think twice on that score).[4] Many artists I encountered referred to the sense of isolation they feel in the heartland. Roger Brown, for example, likens his situation to "the proverbial tree falling in the forest."* Had Phyllis Kind not shown his work in Chicago and later in her New York gallery, he says, ". . .we could have painted our little hearts out and you would have never heard our names or seen one brushstroke of our work." Others view their geographical isolation as a positive fact of existence, even a liberating force. As Hollis Sigler puts it, "You can take risks here out in the 'regions,' you can experiment, you can even fail and no one will point a finger. Besides," she adds only half in jest, "[in many people's minds] you *are*

* Unless otherwise noted, all quotes are taken from the author's interviews with the artists or statements written by the artists for this catalogue.

a failure because you are not in New York." Nicholas Africano admits that he is somewhat ambivalent about his decision to live in Normal, a small town in central Illinois. It was, in part, "a way of reinforcing in myself what has value, what has consequence," he says. He characterizes the New York art scene, particularly in its commercial aspects, as "a race without an end, a race that suggests a kind of transience." He feels the need "to discard that sense of pace" from his life as a working artist and "to be grounded in something that suggests permanence, or at the very least, continuity." Living a good distance from the real or perceived pressures of the marketplace evidently provides him with a certain degree of psychological freedom, not to mention an added measure of solitude that is so crucial to the development of many artists' work.

* * * *

Though all the artists I have selected for this exhibition use recognizable subject matter in their works, they are by no means members of a single coherent movement or an identifiable "ism." Ranging from relatively cool, post-Pop portraits to expressionistic, hallucinatory tableaux, their paintings span a broad stylistic and emotional spectrum. Likewise, a full complement of painterly media is represented in their creations. Included are diminutive watercolors on paper, monumental oil and acrylic paintings on canvas and panel, and exotic hybrids that occupy those grey areas between painting and drawing, and painting and sculpture.

Several artists long associated with Chicago Imagism are represented in this exhibition. Viewers, however, will find very few truly distinguishing marks of regional origin when confronting most of the works in the Biennial. Of course, subject matter occasionally offers a clue, and it is possible to identify artists whose sensibilities are, say, more rural than urban. T. L. Solien's paintings, for example, are filled with references to the wooded, lake-dotted landscape surrounding his Pelican Rapids, Minnesota home. Many of Chicago painter Jim Lutes' works, by contrast, depict the street people he encounters along Milwaukee Avenue where his studio is located. But in most cases, it is virtually impossible to tell without prior information just where most works in the exhibition were made.

Many of the artists' attitudes were shaped in the 1960s and 1970s, two decades characterized by radically different social and aesthetic impulses. As I have noted in another context, if the '60s were synonymous with turbulent social change and a startling parade of "isms" in the visual arts, then the '70s were a time of consolidation, contraction, and introspection—qualities reflected in the self-analytical character of new painting and in an avid new interest in historicism.[5] Not surprisingly, the effects of the philosophical and stylistic contradictions of those decades are evident in many paintings in this exhibition.

Nowhere is this peculiar confluence of style and attitude more apparent than in the work of Kay Miller. A rich amalgam of interests and influences have shaped her art. She considers her paintings "tools for meditation, devices for healing and for restoring vision," reflecting a pantheistic life view that draws on Zen Buddhism, karma yoga, and her own Native American heritage.

Miller's paintings evoke a timeless, spaceless universe in which opposing forces are held in delicate balance. Typically, two recognizable, though greatly abstracted images float, as if unaffected by gravity, within a horizontal field of a single glowing hue. The broadly brushed surfaces are activated by scumbled knots and ridges of paint that radiate from the images like vibrant nuclei and waves of energy.

For Miller, the images are symbols of such basic dualities as east/west, male/female, nature/culture, and she is as interested in their similarities as in their differences. *Vision Quest*, for example, suggests the common ground of Eastern and Native

American spiritualism. Here, a female profile delineated by a schematic diagram of the Eastern system of *chacras* (seats of consciousness) is paired with a bear claw rising from a crescent moon. Miller chose these symbols for their specific meanings and personal associations. She is not concerned that we interpret them in the same light. Rather, she hopes that through their sustained contemplation, viewers will arrive at "a new way of perceiving" and an understanding, as Zen Buddhism teaches, that all apparent opposites are reconciled when viewed as part of a continuous chain.

Of all her themes, Miller has invested the metaphor of travel as life cycle with unexpected vitality and poignancy. Her view of painting as a voyage of personal discovery resonates in the titles of works such as *Scouting*. Similarly, *Deep Sea Diver* refers to her interest in plumbing the depths of her psyche as a means of self-education. In this composition a strand of multi-colored beads floats serenely next to a marine plant whose febrile, flamelike tendrils are buffeted by eddies of paint in the dark blue field. For the artist, both forms represent precious hidden treasures—the nourishment, warmth, and beauty to be found in both nature and humanity—by anyone who embarks, as she puts it, on a "deep *see* voyage."

The journey metaphor persists in *Peace Walk* which was inspired by two events: the birth of a child in her family; and her recent meeting with a group of anti-nuclear protestors who walked solemnly across North America to call attention to their important cause. The painting's brilliant yellow field contains two emblems that, in Miller's mind, suggest generative life forces. On the right stands the Tibetan calligraphic symbol for *om*, the familiar mantra used in the contemplation of ultimate reality. Painted in posteresque shades of red, yellow, green, and white, its sinuous curves are echoed in the thorny arms of the red coral branch that rises beside it. While a clear relationship between these two symbols does not make itself known immediately, delayed speculation suggests several possibilities. For example, the coral branch could be a reference to a tree of life or of knowledge, a fitting counterpart to the glyph whose form resembles a flaming oil lamp, a traditional symbol of enlightenment.

A 1983 painting, *Black Bear Bundle*, is unique within Miller's recent production in that it contains only one image. Set afloat in the infinite space of the red field, the riveting presence of the silhouetted bear commands our attention long after we have walked by the painting. The bear imagery occurs so frequently in Miller's work that upon first seeing this canvas, I wondered if the animal might be an alter ego of sorts for the artist. Always hesitant to discuss specific meanings, Miller replied that she *does* feel certain affinity with the beast who, according to Native American lore, can communicate with all life forms. It is then tempting to view the painting as an oblique self-portrait, for as Miller has written, "through self-identification with an object, one, in a sense, becomes it. This essential oneness of things is the transmutation of the unity of opposites, a realization of spiritual and material forces."[6]

* * * *

Such psychological relationships between viewer and image are equally important to a discussion of Macyn Bolt's art. He describes the fanciful, larger-than-life figures he creates as "emblematic characters from a drama that is continually unfolding." Indeed, upon entering a gallery in which his works are installed, one becomes a participant in a hallucinatory space populated by curious creatures who seem to have sprung onto the walls from another world—the world of dreams and the unconscious.

Bolt is among those young artists for whom Minimalism was the Academy. As a graduate student at Syracuse University, he acquired a facility for producing abstract paintings in the cool, cerebral style that dominated American art for more than a decade. "My work at that time was strictly 'painting about painting,' " he says. Dissatisfied with the rigorously conceptual and impersonal aspects of his austere canvases, and motivated by a desire to "deal with forms that had some greater psychological consequence," he eventually abandoned pure abstraction in favor of figuration.

Since 1981 Bolt has focused on the creation of figurative reliefs composed of modeling paste over layers of carved styrofoam backed by plywood, all enriched with a thick coat of reverberating, expressionistically applied color. These works boldly challenge the limits of traditional painting. The pieces float freely on the wall, yet literally push out into the three-dimensional arena of sculpture and impinge upon the actual space of the viewer.

More anthropomorphic, and sometimes more animal or vegetable than human, Bolt's ambiguous personages evoke a wide range of associations with both popular culture icons and high art sources. Some figures suggest comic book superheroes, among them an exuberant, purple-legged creature with a gaily striped barrel chest. Bolt often reaches deep within himself for more hallucinatory material, offering up images that resemble and have the affecting power of primitive tribal fetishes and ritualistic totems. Although optimism resides in many of his works, his creations are often imbued with a tense, anxious spirit. Frequently, the figures seem at the mercy of potent forces beyond their control. An armless, headless figure, whose calcified surface and indrawn pose suggest a mummified corpse, seems to be eroding. Another figure appears to be undergoing an odd metamorphosis from a human to another, shall we say, more vegetal state. Its flesh sprouts a verdant covering and its sinuous pose suggests a young plant whose leaves are about to unfurl.

Intense and moody, Bolt's works are metaphors for the human condition: for the isolation we may experience; for the tensions, both psychological and physical, that may rule our lives at times; and for the potential of growth and change within us all.

* * * *

No less affecting are the fantastic beings in Robert Lostutter's diminutive watercolors. In these tiny images (each measures 1¾ × 5⅝ inches), two exotic creatures, half-man, half-bird, rise against limitless vistas of tinted space. Within these atmospheric fields, Lostutter's figures materialize with an almost mystical force. Certainly there is a feeling that these characters with their flashing feathers have not been invented as much as conjured out of the vapors by the sheer effort of concentration.

Though Lostutter first gained recognition in the late sixties for monumental paintings on canvas, he has become almost exclusively a watercolorist in the past eight years or so. He had originally hoped that using the watercolor medium would allow him to produce more works than had been possible with the slow, demanding technique he had developed in his oil paintings. Ironically, the watercolors have begun to evolve technical complexities all their own, and he now spends weeks, sometimes months, on even the smallest works. Lostutter builds an image with stroke upon stroke of translucent pigment. Thus, the precise character of a specific color is actually a kind of microscopic pointillism consisting of minute touches of many different hues.[7] The surfaces of these works are so fragile that Lostutter says he must virtually hold his breath while he paints to avoid muddying the colors. (Without a tinge of humor, he notes that a sneeze would be utterly disastrous.)

Lostutter works not only with the finish of a miniaturist but on a scale appropriate to one. Detail is never a superficial embellishment or a needless extravagance. For all their romantic character, there is an innate sense of discipline and restraint to his pictures. Indeed, Lostutter relishes the fact that the gorgeous coloration of his avian creatures is not invented but is a faithful rendition of the actual plumage of hummingbirds he has studied in books, photographs, and drawings.

His figures are imbued with a disquieting combination of majesty and melancholy, poetry and pathos. Who are these creatures? In the artist's view they are emissaries who carry a cautionary missive: a warning that the beauty of the natural world is all too fragile and that we must not destroy it, for if we do, we are, in a sense, destroying ourselves. "We have broken the chain in too many places," Lostutter says. "It's a common message, but it never bores me." But there is more to Lostutter's incorporation of the ravishing products of the natural world with human identity. There is also the suggestion that ". . .there are within us creative factors which can. . .produce marvelous outgrowths of esthetic significance."[8]

Lostutter's recent works refer to diverse art historical traditions. Their scale and meticulous finish suggest medieval illuminations and Persian manuscript paintings. Lostutter admires especially the paintings of the 15th-century Flemish master Rogier van der Weyden, and like that artist, employs a nearly obsessive, painstaking technique. The hallucinatory qualities of his hybrid figures are perhaps closer in spirit to Hieronymus Bosch and, among 20th-century artists, to Richard Lindner who was among his earliest heroes. In that regard and in their immaculately depicted surfaces, his work also bears comparison with that of his Chicago contemporaries, Ed Paschke and Jim Nutt. Yet, for all these associations, Lostutter's vision is thoroughly unique.

At a distance, Lostutter's paintings may be easy to overlook among larger, more robust pictures. As we move in to study them more closely, however, their figures become titanic presences that loom above vaporous clouds. Ultimately, the paintings have an impact that belies their small size, a whispered intensity that is not easy to forget once it has registered.

* * * *

Like Lostutter, Jim Nutt is an *intimiste* whose small-scale paintings display an extraordinary technical virtuosity. When confronting his recent works, we are made aware of powerful polarities within their imagery. Their pinpoint perfection, for instance, is in sharp contrast to their expressive force. We respond to their clarity, evidence of the artist's masterful control of his medium, but are unsettled by their pervasive enigmatic character. "I am interested in the psychological phenomenon of attraction/repulsion," Nutt has said. "It operates on many levels and I think it's part of what gives my work its edge, its ability to command attention."[9]

Nutt's work premiered with the Hairy Who at Chicago's Hyde Park Art Center in 1966. His art seemed to best embody the Who's shocking highbrow/low art aesthetic with its perverse, sometimes vicious humor and its distorted figures rendered in a cartoon-inspired style and hot color.[10] Since those early days, Nutt has continued to produce some of the most compelling and graphically compulsive works of all his Chicago contemporaries. But in recent years he has modulated the high voltage tone of his creations. He has, for example, abandoned the chromatic hedonism of his earlier efforts, and now paints with a limited palette of black, white, and grey.

Works by Nutt in this exhibition can be divided into two categories. Two of the paintings are "invented" portraits in which single figures, gingerly facing the viewer, are set against flat, minimalistic grids. Sure unwavering lines suggesting, on the one hand, the graphic techniques of comic book illustration, and on the other, Attic vase painting, define their clean but distorted features. For all their curvaceous contours, the figures project little sense of

them a certain "Everyman" quality. "I want my portraits to have more than just an effect of something just hanging on a wall. They are always looking at you and you are looking at them," Nechvatal says. Indeed, the spatial and psychological interactions between observer and image are crucial to their effect. The heads' massive scale, sober countenance, and fixed hypnotic stare are riveting. In their vast size and formal pose, they seem more godlike than human.

By his presentation of single, Brobdingnagian faces, Nechvatal's work could be compared with Chuck Close's superscale portrait paintings. Close's work, however, proceeds from a vastly different premise and entails the painterly translation of photographic information onto the canvas. Nechvatal, by contrast, never works from photographs, and ultimately, likeness is of little interest to him. Even those works which depict specific individuals, such as the portrait of his wife Mary, bear only faint resemblance to their subjects. He is involved with such basic painterly issues as light, space, and form, and yet his highly subjective interpretations of his models reveal an impulse to present something more than their surface appearance. In Nechvatal's portraits, identity becomes a container for the human psyche.

* * * *

While exploration of the psyche is the essence of many an artist's approach, Nicholas Africano has taken his to passionate extremes in his work produced since the mid-1970s. At that time, he was making narrative sequences of paintings in which diminutive figures set against expansive fields of uninflected color enact scenes from everyday life. Over the years he has expanded his focus beyond the banalities of daily existence to include metaphorical narratives derived from the world of opera, dance, and literature. As the breadth of his themes has widened, his figures have grown in scale, and now they are usually life-size or larger.

Three sources inspired Africano's recent paintings: *Petrouchka*, the ballet set to music by Igor Stravinsky about a straw puppet with a human heart who longs to be recognized as a man; Fanny Burney's 18th-century novel *Evelina*, the story of a young woman stifled by societal conventions; and various experiences in the artist's own life, including the deaths of his mother and his wife's father. They were people who, Africano says, were "prisoners of appearance or circumstance." The artist refers to this theme as "Angel."

Linking Petrouchka, Evelina, and Angel is a common theme: the conflict between role and will, between outward appearance and inner desire. In his paintings Africano has extracted the characters from their particular narratives and comingled them in new contexts. He thus provides us with a more complete understanding of the essential conflict they share than could be gained by considering each character in isolation.

Africano uses a variety of formal and expressive devices to emphasize his theme. Evoking a sense of the divided self, Petrouchka is depicted both as a straw marionette and as a human dancer whose costume is based on the one worn by Nijinsky in performances of the ballet. Likewise, Evelina appears in some cases fully clothed in a billowing period dress and in others as a vulnerable adolescent nude. The conflict is further echoed in the diptych format and the pictures' paint handling. Typically, each panel carries a single isolated figure rendered in a style that contrasts radically with its companion. In *Dancer and Girl*, for example, the seated Petrouchka is rendered in relief against a pale blue field. His costume, composed of rippling layers of handkerchief linen stiffened with varnish, resin, and paint, literally projects off the canvas surface. To his right is Evelina, whose nude body, painted in thin washes of faint color, dissolves miragelike into the atmospheric field. Color, particularly that of the grounds, functions several ways in these pictures. It suggests simultaneously locale—either interior or exterior—and mood. Furthermore it distances the figures from the viewer in time; dusky pinks, pastel blues, and greens evoke the 18th-century world of such painters as François Boucher and Antoine Watteau.

Perhaps the most subtle, and most successful, expression of the series' central theme is *The Sparrows' Quarrel.* The left panel of this diptych shows Evelina seated gingerly on a white wrought iron chair in a garden defined schematically by the pale green ground; a blooming magnolia bough arches gracefully over her head. At one point, Africano had considered juxtaposing this scene of serenity with a nude whose rather expressionistically painted form would suggest Evelina's internal anger and desires, but his plan changed abruptly. As he explains: "In the summer I tend to spend my mornings outside my studio. One day I saw two sparrows fighting and I sensed within their quarrel something consistent with what I was trying to convey in my paintings. I sensed a proportionate amount of rage and desire built into these frail creatures. Looking at them, I could find no external motive for their behavior; their rage functioned purely on the level of instinct. Instinct, we often assume, amounts to a lost quality in human beings. But perhaps, I thought, instinct is, in fact, expressed within our desires, within our will, that is, within those aspects of our personalities over which we have no intellectual control."

Thus, in the resulting painting, Evelina is juxtaposed with two tiny brown sparrows, their claws extended, wings wildly flapping. Their aggressive behavior is a sharp counterpoint to the calm formality of the seated woman. Evelina seems oblivious to the conflict. Her gloved hands remain primly folded in her lap. Her face, shielded by the wide brim of her picture hat, maintains an impassive expression. In essence, the painting is a metaphor for the willingness with which we accept our roles even though they imply a kind of constraint that amounts to denial of our innermost desires.

In the '70s, Africano often set his paintings in serial arrangements to suggest a disjunctive but nonetheless cinematic unfolding of events through time. In his new work, by contrast, in which he focuses on quintessential moments of spiritual uncertainty, there is little sense of narrative progression. The movement that is implied is not temporal or spatial but emotional—from inner to outer reality and back again. Today his art may speak, as he says, "with a quieter voice," but it still seeks "that strength which equals poise between the truth and the lie." Thus, one thing remains constant in all of Africano's art: his genius in revealing the poetry within the most prosaic experience.

* * * *

Several artists in this exhibition share Africano's interest in exploring themes from literature as well as from their personal history. Prominent among them is T. L. Solien, whose recent paintings are, in essence, scenes from a morality play that reverberate with religious intensity. The fragility of life and the finality of death, the struggle to maintain faith in the face of temptation, and the trials and tribulations of one in search of salvation are their themes. To express these concerns Solien calls into service a host of hapless characters who stumble through life in a harsh and barren landscape not unlike the flat midwestern countryside where he was raised and continues to live.[19] This terrain, he explains, "provides symbols that define me," and even the most hallucinatory images in his paintings often are actually reflections of elements of his immediate environs.

The single most recurrent character in Solien's work is the sad-faced tin man, a creature without a heart who lacks the capacity to feel human emotions. In *Voyage of the Tin Man,* he is lashed to the cruciform mast of a wooden raft balanced precariously on a pile of rocks and split logs. Broken free of its mooring, the boat is propelled across the murky waters by a gust of wind emanating from the mouth of a skull. The painting suggests, on one hand, the passion and sacrifice of a religious martyr. On the other, it may be a commentary on those individuals who journey blindly through life driven not by curiosity and optimism but only by their fear of the inevitability of death.

In other paintings the tin man shares the stage with characters drawn from the illustrated fables in a storybook published in the 1930s that the artist's wife bought for their young daughter. Among these is *The Straw Ox Catches the Devil*, a work inspired by a tale about a poor farm couple who build a straw ox to attract the beasts of the nearby forest so they may use the animals' fur for warmth and their flesh for food. In Solien's painting a cyclopean red devil is stuck to the decoy's tar-covered "hide." The tin man's eyes are tightly closed. Whether he is ignoring or grimacing at the horrific scene is unclear. It is certain, however, that the tin man here represents the artist and that the ox is a metaphor for his painting, the means through which he gains sustenance for his family. Solien also views painting as his means of achieving personal salvation, and he is unsettled that concerns, both good and evil, are potent sources of imagery for him. Thus, we can speculate that the devil is a symbol for the seeds of immorality that Solien recognizes in his otherwise spiritual and moral enterprise.

The autobiographical nature of Solien's storytelling is also evident in *The Sower*, inspired by another fable in his daughter's book. The tale describes the trials of an impoverished peasant boy who goes to the North Wind to retrieve the grain she has blown out of his bowl. In his painting Solien departs from the story's plot and focuses instead on the apple-cheeked youth. The boy is rendered in a simplified style that closely approximates the storybook illustration. Beside him the head of the tin man and a ghoulish skull rest against the trunk of a denuded tree. For Solien, the painting is a representation of the three ages of man, with the tin man being a self-portrait of the artist at mid-life, wistfully recalling his youth and contemplating his death. Tears and rocks suggesting the burdens of life rain from the ominous sky onto the parched earth and heighten the poignant melancholy of the tableau.

To convey his narratives, Solien has developed a highly personal, identifiable style that draws on aspects of several art forms. He and his wife have a large collection of primitive folk toys, whose elemental shapes often resonate in the naive rendering of his figures. The visionary spatial realms of Surrealism also seem to have a bearing on his art, as do the late works of Philip Guston, in which eerie landscapes are inhabited by creatures who are at once grotesque and beguiling.

Solien's achievement is twofold. He has the ability to describe stories that, however private their significance, burrow beneath our consciousness and open a Pandora's box of universal associations. At the same time, we respond to the quality of his painting, to the conviction with which simple images are transformed into compelling visual experiences.

* * * *

Hollis Sigler's art, like Solien's, is essentially autobiographical and narrative. As a student at the School of The Art Institute of Chicago, she became increasingly disturbed by the cool impersonality of the photorealist pictures she was making. Abandoning painting, she sought new formal and expressive possibilities in her childhood pastime of drawing. The change of medium was liberating. Drawing as she had as a child, "without skill, without perspective, without proportion, without passing judgment," she discovered, allowed her to express herself more directly. "I found that I was dealing with my interior space," she says, "describing in images how I felt at the moment, rather than dealing with things outside myself."

Sigler eventually worked her way back to painting, retaining the naive, even childlike style she had developed in her drawings. The canvases she has produced in recent years depict various episodes in the life of a woman who Sigler usually refers to only as "the lady" or "she." They chronicle her innermost thoughts in moments of pain, joy, or desperation. While there is a high quotient of fantasy in these works, Sigler acknowledges that they are based loosely on events in her own life and that "the lady" is her alter ego.

In the past Sigler tended to set her theatrical vignettes in moody, claustrophobic interiors suggesting the deep recesses of the mind. Now she often depicts lush tropical landscapes not unlike those she explored on a recent trip in the Caribbean. Through her imaginative transformations these, too, become hallucinatory stage sets of the unconscious in which psychological dramas are played out. Their central theme is desire, "the lady's" hopes of transcending the banalities of daily existence.

Her fantasies, her dreams of romance and glamour, are symbolized in several paintings by a silhouetted figure wearing a black evening gown. The figure is tall and elegant but spectral; the lack of definition of her features suggests just how elusive desire can be. In *Vessi d'Ignato Amor* (To Live with a Hidden Love), she has escaped the confines of the dark and gloomy painter's studio that fills the foreground of the canvas. Champagne glass in hand, she dances in the sunlight beyond a diaphanous curtain. She appears again in *Desire Released*, waltzing through an exotic landscape. Her silhouetted profile looms against the full moon and is reflected in the rippling waters that lap at the base of the cliffs which bracket the dreamlike scene.

Sigler's most successful paintings are those in which the sensuous forms and rich tonalities of the landscape embody the woman's passion and sense of emotional release. Among these works is *Mysterious Delights of the Heart*, in which nervous lines and staccato strokes of brilliant color define the scintillating sea and sky and the palm-studded cliffs that frame the composition. A generalized golden luminosity suffuses the scene and heightens its idyllic character. The motley campsite in the foreground, with its tent, clothesline, and suburban plastic lounge chair, injects a humorous note of reality into the otherwise arcadian vision.

The artist's primitivistic style reflects her admiration, as she says, "of naive artists, those without formal schooling, without the influence of Europe, but whose work [is] alive and accessible." There is a certain deliberate and sure quality to her facile touch that belies this expressed anti-academic stance. Her jewel-toned palette and loving, obsessively painstaking attention to surface detail suggest comparison with the paintings of the Italian master Simone Martini, who was among her earliest influences. Her use of landscape as a vehicle for expressing intense emotional states also relates her thinking to the romantic mentality of such 19th-century American painters as Thomas Cole, whose work she greatly admires.

Sigler's works, however, are by no means archaistic. In several aspects—their handmade frames, which lend the paintings an objectlike quality, and certainly their highly personal subject matter—they relate to the creations of several artists in this exhibition. Ultimately, Sigler speaks with her own voice, one which tells of the mysteries of the soul and the beauties of the natural world.

* * * *

Michael Nakoneczny's works, like Sigler's, are visual diaries that chronicle his emotional responses to various events in his life. In the past three years he has developed a confident and consistent style, producing small-scale paintings on masonite panels set in weathered wood or beaten metal frames.

Nakoneczny begins each work by carefully applying a coat of gesso to the masonite surface. From then on, his technique is strictly intuitive and improvisational. "I start with a mood," he explains, "then I begin scribbling or slopping on paint or laying down washes of color with rags or big brushes. That gives me clues and then I just let the painting pull me along." As he continues to work, recognizable images—figures, animals, buildings—emerge out of the dense accretion of pictographic scribbles and amorphous smudges of paint. He refines their forms, fleshing them out with color, outlining them with wavering strokes of black paint, and giving them more specific attributes. "The images become the ideas," Nakoneczny says, "and a dialogue begins. . . . When all the elements have had their say, the painting is done."

The resulting paintings are jam-packed with wildly distorted figures, whose graphic crudity recalls children's drawings, the art of the insane, and the graffiti that appears on urban building facades. Nakoneczny says that the busy, energetic surfaces of his works reflect his view of contemporary life: "The world is very crazy—the TV's on, cars are going by, children are running around—you can't sort it out." Indeed, his paintings are visions of sensory overload. Typical is *Crossing Wires*, which was inspired by a series of particularly trying days in his life. The composition is dominated by a portrait of the artist surrounded by dozens of smaller figures, wildly flailing their arms, yacking into telephones. Beside him is a scrawled caption "1,000 people talking" and emblazoned on his cheek is the head of a crowing rooster that suggests the intensity of the oral and visual cacophony by which he is bombarded.

For all their superficial crudity, there is a kind of beauty about Nakoneczny's paintings. Upon close inspection, their surfaces, like sections of old walls, are subtly, even sensuously modulated. And as in the works of Jean Dubuffet, who the artist admires, there is a certain enchantment in their chaotic splendor.

* * * *

Peter Huttinger's enigmatic narratives and images evolve out of a process of free association similar to Nakoneczny's work. "I want my works to be dialogues that involve the viewer in the turmoil and doubt that I experience in making them," he says.

Huttinger, who began his career as a ceramist, has in recent years produced a large body of work that includes drawings, paintings, sculptures, and mixed media pieces that are hybrid combinations of these. His freewheeling approach is a reflection of his diverse interests, which span the history of art and popular culture. Japanese pottery, funk ceramics, folk art, underground comics, graffiti, Dada, Surrealism, Abstract Expressionism, the Hairy Who, Minimalism—all these have had a bearing, he says, on the development of his multi-faceted sensibility. These are cited not to suggest that Huttinger's work is only a synthesis of styles but rather to characterize the divergent formal and expressive territories with which it connects.

Huttinger's works in this exhibition are multipanel compositions of drawings cum paintings on paper. Their imagery derives from the artist's view of his own personal experiences and relationships, as well as his reflections on topics ranging from the "taboo" of sex and violence to the sublime, religion. To express those concerns, he draws from a reservoir of personal symbols, among them the dagger, the vase, the rabbit, and also appropriates images from art historical and popular culture sources. These are combined in such a way that it is often only after lengthy consideration that the totality of their significance becomes clear to the viewer. Our attempts to analyze their meanings are impeded further by Huttinger's method of layering one image over another. This technique provides the surfaces of his works with a lively and continuous sense of animation that is analogous to the stream of conscious process by which they are generated.

While many of Huttinger's works deal with such tough and anxious subject matter as racial conflict, urban violence, and nuclear war, the recent birth of his son has inspired a group of more optimistic pieces. The most ambitious and complex of these is *Lots*, which consists of nine drawings/paintings set in a grid. As its title suggests, *Lots* is filled with a wealth of imagery, all of which is related to themes of fertility and growth.

At the four corners of the composition is the face of a bucktoothed rabbit, a traditional symbol of fecundity, whose eyes are formed of wilting tulips and ears metamorphose into pink-nippled breasts. The rabbit's face is repeated again in large scale as a spare graphite drawing that extends across the nine panels of the piece. Superimposed over it are nine vases, some of which hold tulips. Huttinger stresses the figurative qualities of these vessels, accentuating their curves and using color to endow each with its own specific character and attributes. The bulbous vase with pendulous breasts at the center of the bottom row, for example, resembles the Venus of Willendorf, the ancient fertility goddess. A subtle pattern of sinuous vines, a motif traditionally symbolic of eternal life, energizes the entire surface and draws together the various images.

In discussing *Lots*, Huttinger explains that behind the work is a complex iconographic program based on his own as well as traditional religious symbolism. Its title, he notes, refers in part to the biblical story of Lot, a moral man living in the corrupt city of Sodom. The work's compositional format also has symbolic connotations that stem from Renaissance religious painting. The top tier of drawings represents the metaphysical/heavenly plane, the middle tier refers to the plane of intellect, and the lower tier symbolizes the realm of earthly senses. Huttinger is not concerned, however, that viewers share his personal interpretations of the piece. As he explains, "I am more interested in the emotional impact of a work of art than what it does on a formal or cognitive level."

By their stream of conscious combination of imagery, Huttinger's works may be viewed as contemporary manifestations of the Surrealist "exquisite corpse." Furthermore, his creations, like those of Jim Nutt who he admires, are both off-putting and engaging. A single work may contain images as appealing as an Indonesian shadow puppet, academically rendered in meticulous detail, and as bizarre and unsettling as an aggressively distorted nude covered with feces and viscera. Reflecting his training as a ceramist, Huttinger is adept at developing a variety of rich textural surfaces. In *Lots*, for example, some of the vessels have a smooth, almost enameled perfection. Others, stained by glue and pocked by eraser dust ground into the paper, suggest comparison with the bruised and abraded surfaces of Joseph Beuys' drawings. It is precisely these contradictory qualities which give Huttinger's works their strength. In their bizarre collisions of images and conflicting styles, his works jar our sensibilities, and in so doing, they are all the more memorable.

* * * *

For Jim Lutes, as for so many artists in this exhibition, "narrative content is not an end in itself; [rather it] serves as a vehicle for the emotions." The scenes he portrays, he says, "are born of experience and direct observation, but are painted from memory and are somehow bent and twisted in the process."

Lutes studied at Washington State University before attending the School of The Art Institute in Chicago where he continues to live. He feels no particular affinity with any artistic tradition of the area, describing himself not as a Chicago artist but "as an artist who happens to live in Chicago." He acknowledges, however, that his work is intimately connected to the environment in which it is produced. It has a gritty edge to it that evokes the grim realities of the tough urban neighborhood in which he lives. Frequently, Lutes portrays the "street people" he encounters near his studio. *Mr. Business*, for example, is a hybrid portrait in which he combined the suited figure of a local merchant with the pockmarked, red-veined face of an old wino who lives on Milwaukee Avenue, a section of which forms the background of the painting.

To create his paintings, Lutes employs a method not unlike that used by Michael Nakoneczny. He begins each work by applying thin washes and daubs of paint to the canvas surface, selecting their hues to evoke his feelings about a particular person, event, or set of circumstances in his life. As he studies the amorphous field, forms suggesting buildings, people, animals, and so on begin to emerge. Lutes then defines their specific characteristics with more deliberate strokes of color.

Lutes' works in this exhibition can be divided into three categories. The first consists of "street pictures" such as *Mr. Business.* A second is comprised of surrealistic "memory portraits," among them *Death and the Bulldog*, which is based on reminiscences of a childhood pet. An ominous mood prevails in this nightscape in which a small canine is silhouetted against a snow covered street. The animal confronts the viewer directly, unaware of the approaching auto whose hood emerges miragelike from the broadly painted white ground.

Works in the third category portray scenes in Lutes' studio, which occupies the second floor of a crumbling ninety-year-old building. These include a compelling portrait of the artist, surely among his most successful works to date. The painting occupied Lutes for several months, yet there is a startling freshness and immediacy about the portrait in which the artist confronts us directly, "warts and all," revealing his rather shabby work environment. As is his practice, Lutes began this painting by "trying to capture the sense of myself through abstract, gestural forms," and it was only late in the process of its creation that he studied his features in a mirror. In its delicate balance of abstraction and description, the painting retains a sense of the process by which it was generated. The artist's sober face, with its two-day growth of beard, is rendered in meticulous detail. The cracked and peeling studio wall, by contrast, is described in a much looser, gestural fashion. Its broadly painted patches of swirling color are in sharp counterpoint to the severe geometries of the window to its right through which a view of the street strewn with garbage is visible. To evoke the environment depicted in the painting, Lutes has set the portrait in a heavy frame constructed of weathered wood molding scavenged from an old building in his neighborhood. This frame calls further attention to the painting as an object (a technique used by several other artists in this exhibition) and invests the work with a level of actuality beyond the painted imagery.

* * * *

The struggle for self-revelation that characterizes the work of so many artists in this exhibition is given especially potent expression in the art of John Broenen. As a student at the University of Wisconsin in Milwaukee, he produced abstract paintings before turning to figuration in an attempt to "find more personal subject matter." His first works in that mode were odd little paintings on panels or scraps of paper whose surfaces teem with Boschian creatures. Broenen found this foray into the realm of pure fantasy inconclusive and eventually turned to his own life for subject matter.

In the past two years he has produced an impressive series of large-scale paintings. Though inspired by personal experiences and dreams, they are not specifically narrative. Rather, they are visual allegories of the artist's mental landscape. The setting for many of these hallucinatory scenes is the artist's childhood home. Broenen describes its rooms and hallways with rapid-fire, expressionistic strokes of high keyed color that transform the house into a technicolor "Cabinet of Dr. Caligari."

When viewing Broenen's expansive canvases at close range, we become virtually lost in their dense networks of luscious color. The paintings are seductively beautiful, although their subjects are often disturbing. Consider *The Squeeze Man*, in which the artist's severed head sits on a table in a room whose walls loom and jut at odd angles. In a nearby doorway Broenen's decapitated body stands, or rather floats, for his feet have been severed as well. The slashing strokes of red, yellow, and green paint with which the interior is described heighten the sense of violence in this gruesome tableau. An element of comic relief is provided, however, by the cocky little dog who stands beneath the table.

Broenen is at his best when the violence he portrays is more psychological than physical, as in *Conversations with Plants.* Its setting is the artist's bedroom which, through Broenen's imaginative transformations, becomes a surreal dream space. Its surfaces are knit together with parallel strokes of vivid yellow and green hues that glow and coruscate with an eerie light. Broenen lies in a coffin-shaped bed at the foot of which is an armless mannequin who seems somehow more alive than the artist himself. The most animated presence in the room, however, is a potted plant suspended from the ceiling. Its sinuous vines snake about the space, looping around the window valence, through the horns of the cow skull hanging on the wall, until they finally coil around the artist's neck.

In style and spirit Broenen's art may be viewed as a manifestation of the expressionist tradition, which extends in this century from such early practitioners as Emil Nolde and Ernst Ludwig Kirchner to the generation of contemporary German painters that includes Walter Dahn and Helmut Middendorf. It is, however, van Gogh with whom Broenen feels the greatest affinity. Indeed, confronting his paintings we recall the post-impressionist master's statement that he "tried to express the terrible passions of humanity by means of red and green."

* * * *

The durable spirit of expressionism inhabits the work of several artists in this exhibition. Prominent among them is Lance Kiland, for whom painting is an improvisational affair with mystical overtones. He rarely makes preliminary sketches, preferring instead to work directly on the canvas and to paint, as he says, with as few preconceptions as possible. Often his original notions for a picture fall away as he lets his involvement with the painting process dictate the forms that appear in the finished work. "I might have something specific in mind, but the painting fights back," Kiland explains. "It's as though there is a mysterious element in the paint that communicates the subject to me. It's almost a primal transmission. It can't be ignored."

Kiland builds up his canvases with layer upon layer of thick oil paint into which a generous dose of wax has been mixed. As he paints "wet into wet," recognizable forms—arms, heads, torsos—often materialize within the expressionistic flow of color. Occasionally, he "erases" these emergent images with another layer of paint, only to find that some of them reappear within the increasingly crusty strata. A firm believer in "the value of accepting the inevitable," Kiland ultimately allows the most stubbornly recurrent images to capture his attention. At that point, his method becomes more analytical than intuitive. Now he models the forms with deliberate strokes of the brush and often defines their contours with bold black lines. He works over the entire surface, carefully readjusting the formal and expressive relationships between the images.

The resulting paintings are quasi-narrative tableaux filled with figures and plantlike forms that seem in a constant state of flux. Recalling to some extent Willem de Kooning's women, the images in Kiland's works struggle to emerge from dense thickets of abstract markings and gestural passages of paint. Luminous hues of vibrant pinks and aquas, and throbbing reds and oranges define both figure and ground. Here and there, broad swaths of color extend across the black lines that begin to separate the figures from the surrounding space, only to turn and knife through them at arbitrary angles.

Several paintings are dominated by figures that seem chiseled out of stone. In *New Life*, for example, a budding plant and a truncated torso resembling sculptures in the early stages of carving are perched on a raft. For all their rock hard solidity, these enigmatic, contorted entities seem somehow alive, as the title suggests. Energetic brushwork invigorates their faceted surfaces and imbues these petrified *personnages* with a burgeoning sense of organic growth. Or consider *Torsos*, a view of an artist's studio filled with sculptural fragments. Here, two armless statues become aggressive, muscular presences that appear to be trying to raise themselves out of the very material that defines them. The intensity of their struggle reverberates in the frenzied paint handling of the surrounding space which pulsates with virtually palpable energy.

Kiland's paintings are frequently compared to the work of his young Italian contemporaries. The luscious palette, sensuous textures, and monumentality of the "classical" figures in such canvases as *Torsos* and *Divining Rod* do, in fact, call to mind the paintings of Sandro Chia. It is important to note, however, that Kiland's involvement with expressionistic figuration predates his knowledge of the Italian artist's work. As Eleanor Heartney has observed, there are significant differences between their creations, most importantly that "Kiland's figures are not burdened with the dead weight of history nor are they haunted by cultural ghosts. One cannot imagine them trudging endlessly up the mountain of regret like Chia's Sisyphus."[20]

Indeed, Kiland's compelling images spring more from his imagination than from any art historical or mythological source. His figures that raise themselves from the chaos of paint are visual metaphors for the very process of creation. They embody Kiland's "ongoing effort to wrest meaning from his medium."[21]

* * * *

Tom Keesee's paintings in this exhibition represent a new direction in the evolution of his art. For several years, urban architecture was the point of departure for his work. In an extended series of diminutive panel paintings he depicted the facades of buildings near his downtown Indianapolis studio with thickly impastoed strokes of paint. These were followed by a group of portraits of friends and family members. More emotionally charged than his cityscapes, these gesturally painted images suggest Keesee's growing interest in going beyond a simple imitative rendering of reality to probe more subjective, hallucinatory realms.

Recently, Keesee abandoned the constraints of direct observation in favor of a more improvisational approach that has allowed him to expand the range of his imagery significantly. Now, like Lance Kiland, he relies on the process of painting to generate his subjects, which include invented portraits and multi-figure compositions that allude to historical and biblical narratives.

Whereas his earlier paintings were executed in a relatively rapid way, Keesee now spends several weeks on each canvas. He builds up their images with numerous layers of thick oil paint that ultimately encase the entire surface like a heavy crust. In *The Flood*, for example, the figures seem unable to escape neither the roily waters that engulf them nor the turbid paint that delineates them. Similarly, the broad strokes and scumbled ridges of muddy color that form the angst-ridden visage of the figure in *The Professor* never completely lose their identity as passages of pure pigment. This subtle balance between the abstract and descriptive qualities of paint is a hallmark of Keesee's style.

Like many young artists today, Keesee feels a deep affinity with the early 20th-century expressionists. He admires particularly the work of Georges Rouault, whose influence is evidenced in the pervasive and eerie blue tonality of many of Keesee's canvases and in his use of broken black lines to define the angular contours of his aggressively distorted figures. The art of Emil Nolde would also seem to have a bearing on Keesee's work. The masklike visage and raw sensuality of the naked female figure in his painting *Adam and Eve* call to mind Nolde's *Maria Aegyptica*.

A whiff of Surrealism is also found about Keesee's work. Consider, for example, *The Whispering,* which is among his most riveting and enigmatic paintings to date. This work began, the artist explains, as a depiction of Charlemagne's coronation by the pope. In the process of painting, however, Keesee transformed the emperor into a medieval stone sculpture and replaced the pontiff with a demonic creature. Resembling a gargoyle come to life, the red beast clings to the sculpture's back and, despite the title's explanation of the scene, his action is ambiguous. On the one hand, the creature appears to be trying to breathe life into the mute sculpture. On the other, there is the suggestion of something more macabre and sinister; perhaps the beast is trying to devour the figure.

* * * *

Ken Nevadomi's paintings are eclectic fusions of several styles and sensibilities. Though formally rooted in the expressionist painterly tradition, elements of pop, surrealism, and social realism are also detectable in his work. When asked with which tradition he feels the greatest affinity, Nevadomi replies, "I'm less concerned with Art than with a vision. I'm not entirely sure what the vision is or where it is leading me, and I may never know. What is interesting to me is looking for it."

Nevadomi's paintings in this exhibition suggest the divergent directions his quest has taken him in recent years. Discussing their sources, he has said, "Everything is grist for the mill. I paint from historical, literary, or political sources, or from impulse. I try to internalize my experiences and what I know of other people's experience. Also, I fantasize about what I read, hear, see (or think I see) . . . stir this up in my brain and let it out on the canvas."

The resulting paintings range from fanciful to frightening, from dreamy to nightmarish scenes that make potent commentary on the grim realities of contemporary life. Among works in the latter category is *Political Deviant with Keeper,* which was inspired by media accounts of the brutal treatment of prisoners in Central America. Here, within a shallow cell-like space, a beefy, bare-chested thug with a maniacal grin shoves a straight-jacketed man into a box with a metal grate for a cover. The gestural rendering of the figures and the dramatic diagonal shadows that knife through the space heighten the sense of violence in this horrific scene.

Nevadomi's thinking is characterized by outrageous leaps of imagination, and in several works he pushes artistic license into distant corners. Witness *Hitler in Hell,* one of a series of paintings in which Nevadomi speculates on the Führer's activities in the afterlife. The top half of the painting is a turbulent blue field energized by broad strokes and squiggles of lurid color suggesting stygian chaos. Below, in a cubic space frame recalling the airless settings of Francis Bacon's psychological dramas, an improbable meeting is taking place: Hitler, seated in a comfy, floral-patterned armchair, pours out his heart to Sigmund Freud, who madly scribbles his thoughts on a notepad.

Occasionally, Nevadomi unleashes his mordant wit on subjects grounded in the history of art, and not surprisingly, his renditions of traditional themes are characteristically irreverant. A series of paintings based on the story of Adam and Eve is a case in point. "I've always been bothered by those paintings of Eden that make the place look like a valley in Pennsylvania," Nevadomi quips. Thus, in *Adam and Eve Dance with the Animals*, he describes paradise in something less than idyllic terms. Nothing is static in this chaotic landscape. The heads of two deities rage across the sky like ominous thunderheads. Rendered in staccato strokes of pulsing red, yellow, and blue paint, the turbulent atmosphere provides an emotional counterpoint to the frenzied dance of the exuberant figures below.

* * * *

As this exhibition attempts to illustrate, regionalism is no longer a significant factor in painting in the United States. The work of the seventeen artists on view here clearly testifies to the vitality of painting in the Midwest. But as I have tried to demonstrate, there is, with few exceptions, nothing specifically midwestern about their imagery. The artists' concerns transcend geographical boundaries, and if anything, their varied creations reflect what is not a regional but rather an international phenomenon: the proliferation of divergent representational styles that characterize painting today.

1. For a discussion of Ohio's art scene, see the exhibition catalogue, *Outside New York: The State of Ohio* (The New Museum of Contemporary Art, New York, 1980).

2. Russell Bowman, "Chicago Imagism: The Movement and the Style," *Who Chicago?* (Sunderland Arts Centre, Ltd., 1980), 28.

3. Dennis Adrian, "Introduction," *Chicago: Some Other Traditions* (Madison Art Center, Madison, Wisconsin, 1983), 9.

4. The district's major thoroughfares are Superior and Huron.

5. Lisa Lyons, *The Anxious Edge* (Walker Art Center, Minneapolis, 1982), 4.

6. From a statement by the artist in *New Work: New York/ Outside New York* (The New Museum of Contemporary Art, New York, 1984), 47.

7. Dennis Adrian, *Robert Lostutter: The Watercolors* (The Renaissance Society at the University of Chicago, 1984), 7.

8. *Ibid.*, 8.

9. Russell Bowman, "An Interview with Jim Nutt," *Arts Magazine* (March 1978), 135.

10. Dan Cameron, "Nutt's Progress," *Arts Magazine* (April 1984), 66.

11. John Yau, *Jim Nutt: Recent Works* (The Mayor Gallery, London, 1983), np.

12. Bowman, *op. cit.*, 135.

13. Mitchell Douglas Kahan, "Roger Brown and the American Scene," *Roger Brown* (Montgomery Museum of Fine Arts, 1980), 9.

14. Dennis Adrian, "Roger Brown and the Chicago Context," *Roger Brown* (Montgomery Museum of Fine Arts, 1980), 35.

15. Jack Cowart, *Currents 6: Roger Brown* (St. Louis Art Museum, 1980), np.

16. Russell Bowman, "Roger Brown: Style and Emblem," *Roger Brown* (Montgomery Museum of Fine Arts, 1980), 28.

17. Dennis Adrian in *Ed Paschke* (The Renaissance Society at the University of Chicago, 1982), 10.

18. Ed Paschke, "Notes on a Work in Progress," *Profile: Ed Paschke*, III, No. 5 (September 1983), 29.

19. Marge Goldwater, "T. L. Solien," *Images and Impressions: Painters Who Print* (Walker Art Center, Minneapolis, 1984), 52.

20. Eleanor Heartney, "Lance Kiland," *Arts Magazine* (January, 1984), 6.

21. *Ibid.*, 6.

# NICHOLAS AFRICANO

---

**Journal Entry: The Surrender, 1975**

I fear and envy the one who only loves danger. The one who is not afraid of what is wrong; who is ruthless and without grace.

One cannot choose to be innocent.

But the one who is elegantly cynical may not weather the storm of anxious desire that waits.

**Journal Entry: Petrouchka, work in progress, 1983–84**

(Recall: *The Surrender,* 1975)

I fear and envy the one who is not afraid of what is wrong; who is ruthless and without grace.

**From a letter to Kushner, 1984**

Glenn Johnson died; Cynthia and I have a son, my dear Nicholas Johnson; we have a home; my mother Anna died. These events are so very ordinary when applied to the experience of one in his early middle age.

But in these years I have withdrawn, never allowed my life and my art to touch, to meet with real consequence.

I feel no loss in that: my paintings from these years are made with a curious ardor, a displaced passion that is intrinsic to them. They are an authentic response to a life in which I had no sense of place.

I am only a little less bewildered by life's common ironies, but a kind of integration is occurring within my own life that I hope will reveal itself in my art as well. It is a harsh movement, not poetic in its progress.

My art will speak with a quieter voice; and seek that strength which equals poise between the truth and the lie.

*Conversations with Plants*, 1983, checklist no. 11

# ROGER BROWN

## On the Perils of Being an Artist in the Midwest

Lisa Lyons interviewed all of us for her essay which I am sure will tell more about my work than I could say in a few words. Instead, I'll tell you what it's like to be a living, breathing, human being/ artist in the Midwest.

Well, if it weren't for Phyllis Kind and her gallery, it would be like the proverbial tree falling in the forest—we could have painted our little hearts out and you would have never heard our names or seen one brushstroke of our work. No doubt, Phyllis and I have had our differences, but we have also had our agreements, and she is one hell of an art dealer.

So she took us out of the desert of the Midwest art press and into the promised land of *Artforum*. In my naivete a long time ago, I made the "mistake" of going to Chicago instead of heading for the New York Art World. Hell, I didn't even know there was an art world much less where it was. But Phyllis went there for all of her artists who were working away in this desert and were just pleased to be doing our thing and selling enough work to keep going. What more can you ask than to make a living at what you really enjoy doing?

But then we became known. Phyllis took us to New York and we got Famous. Do you know what it's like to get famous outside your own hometown? You know that book that says you can't go home again? You can't just stay home either. Do you have any idea what it's like to succeed in a town where others remained and failed? I mean we stayed here, folks!—no trotting off to the East Coast to become another art star. We dared to stay in Chicago, and boy, do they hate us for it. Who's "they?" "They" are the museum Joneses trying to keep up with the museum Smiths; "they" are failed artist, Franz Schulze, trying to be an art critic, and failed music critic, Alan Artner, pretending to "see" as an art critic; "they" are artists who stayed in Chicago but imitated New York styles until those styles became passé. Then, too, there are the editors of Chicago's yellow art journal, *The New Art Examiner*. God, can you believe it? The only art magazine from Chicago is like *The National Enquirer* or *Hustler*.

I've had people here in Chicago talk of knowing what my work is all about. Some say they *know* my work hasn't grown. But do you know something? They don't even know that they haven't seen any of my work in a gallery show in Chicago in five years—since 1979 (that is about one hundred paintings). Frankly, showing in Chicago is like hiding your light under a bushel.

I know that because of my having had success, all this is supposed to roll off my back like water off a duck. You gotta really be tough-minded in this town. Not to worry—I'm tough enough—but is anybody in Chicago listening? Or looking? Writers? Editors? Publishers? Museum administrators? Anybody?

Chicago, 1984

*Seeking Shelter*, 1984, checklist no. 19

# PETER HUTTINGER

---

This poem, written by Tex Williams, a folk artist and lyricist who lives in Cincinnati, Ohio, was inspired by Peter Huttinger's work.

### My Bunny

by
Tex Williams, Lyricist
December 8, 1983

My Bunny Happy—Pokes up her head.
From the that she calls home ϰ
When I am with her—happy happy,
ner do wish to roam ϰ

•:•

She soft hair I run in my Fingers.
As my Bunny I caress ϰ
With her tulips—as For eyes.
Lovely Breast are For eyes ϰ

•:•

Most White as Her Fur as others not.
For Her Fur be color of sun—yellow ϰ
No squeak her voice—so soft,
but tis quietly, beautiful, mellow ϰ

•:•

As many Fools will say tis strange.
That one Has yellow Bunny For thy Friend ϰ
But I know that they that speak so.
Are Fickle—My Bunny is mine till the end ϰ

Finis

*Peace Walk*, 1984, checklist no. 46

# MICHAEL NAKONECZNY

---

When I paint I try to shut up the internal chatter and scribble out images as blindly as possible. The images become the ideas and a dialogue begins. I try not to manipulate the characters presented but let them tell their own story. The painting is built on chaotic stops and starts. When all elements have had their say, the painting is done.

*Crossing Wires*, 1984, checklist no. 49

# DENNIS NECHVATAL

---

## NOWISM

STATUES FALLING
HELL'S FLYING IN LOW AND UNSURE
YELLOW HEAD SCREAMS AND REACHES
PARTED LIPS OPEN WIDE
A MESSAGE FROM SILVER SHADOW
HELP!
PRIMITIVE CONTEMPORARY OF PUFFY COLORS
TURNS NEON RED UNDER NUDE MASK
CLOUDS ARE OUT OF PLACE
I JUST CAN'T MAKE OUT WHAT IS GOING ON INSIDE
A DAY CHANGES
GREEN MAN OVER LIVE EYE
A SCREENING
TODAY IS STRANGE ISN'T IT
A CYCLE OF ALL NATURES
A MOVEMENT OF LEVELS
SPIRITUAL SHIFTING
TRANCED FORMS CAUGHT IN TIME
PRACTICE LIFE
THOUGHTS PILED UP FROM EXPERIENCE
ONE EXPERIENCE CRASHES INTO ANOTHER
IMAGE OF ICEBERGS ON RED SEA
ON THE SHORES FALLEN HALOS
THE EDGES ARE ON FIRE
I SEE THE ARM OF THE GOLDEN PAST TURN FLESH
REALITY IS THROWN
BACK TO THE ABSTRACT
WHILE RIDGED PEOPLE FLOAT BY

STATUES ARE FALLING

*Mary*, 1983, checklist no. 55

# KEN NEVADOMI

At the artist's request, no statement is printed.

*Adam and Eve Dance with the Animals*, 1983, checklist no. 57

# JIM NUTT

---

At the artist's request, no statement is printed.

*Observe the conVeNient Excuse*, 1984, checklist no. 65

# ED PASCHKE

---

The idea of electronically translating life has been an intriguing concept to me for some time. Computer graphics, digital read-outs, X-ray, and the scan-lined video image have all influenced my way of seeing. Impressions, gestures, and impulses viewed through the look of artificial intelligence have become part of our visual language. My paintings, therefore, address themselves to this dialogue between Nature and Technology.

*Jupiter*, 1983, checklist no. 67

# HOLLIS SIGLER

Several years ago I, for the most part, stopped using paint. Instead, my creative energies were focused in my journals, writings about my life, what was happening to me, around me, and there were drawings, too. Soon I just was doing these drawings. They were so satisfying to me! They were immediate, accessible, like the drawings of my childhood. I was no longer *thinking* so hard, not laboring over my work. I found that I was making drawings about my life, me, and that they were fun to do and spontaneous. At the same time these drawings filled a hole in my personality. I found that I was expressing myself more accurately, and this is what I needed. I used only childhood materials then. Because of my familiarity with them, they provided the ease to get where I wanted to go. Nothing truly technical got in my way. Then after years of exploration, I started to work in paint again. I still have a "romance" with paint. I couldn't let go so easily.

Now around me, the external influences were the Chicago School and Dubuffet. Dubuffet told us that there was something valid in the work of children and the disturbed. And we observed the local naive artists, those without formal schooling and the influence of Europe, whose works were alive and accessible, using knowledge of the self as their inspiration.

I'm still exploring what I set out to do back then, using the ability to paint spontaneously to explore my life through painting here in Chicago. Perhaps all the reasons are not clear to me, but I feel freer here.

*Mysterious Delights of the Heart*, 1983, checklist no. 71

# T.L. SOLIEN

---

And while I cover the distance that separates me from the coffin, looking at my men, impassive, sitting on the bed, I feel that I've breathed in the first breath of air that boils up over the dead man, all that bitter matter that destroyed Macondo.

Gabriel Garcia Marquez, "The Leaf Storm," *The Leaf Storm and Other Stories* (Harper and Row Publishers, Inc., New York, 1972).

Because I feel there is no heaven on earth,
because I desire my work to be responsive to the act of living as a human being,
because I am of the devil as I am of God,
because I am a Mortal,
because I feel there is more,
my work is like this.

T.L. Solien, 1984

A big bear
came out of the woods.
The bear looked at the ox and said,
"Who are you?
Tell me, who are you?"
The straw ox said,
"Oh! I am just an ox
made of straw and tar."
Then the bear said,
"My fur is ragged.
I must have some straw and tar.
I must patch my ragged fur."
"Take some," said the ox.
The bear started to pull away
some straw and tar.
He pulled, and pulled, and pulled.
He could not pull away
the straw and tar.
He could not pull himself away.

"The Straw Ox," *I Know a Story* (Row, Peterson and Company, New York, Evanston, and San Francisco, 1938).

*The Sower*, 1984, checklist no. 77

# CHECKLIST OF THE EXHIBITION

Dimensions are given in inches; height precedes width precedes depth.

* Washington only
** Washington and Evanston only

## Nicholas Africano

All works are mixed media on canvas; and unless otherwise indicated, courtesy Holly Solomon Gallery, New York.

1. *Dancer and Girl* 1984
   2 parts, 72 × 48 each
   Collection Laila and Thurston Twigg-Smith
2. *Evelina* 1984
   2 parts, 84 × 60 and 12 × 9
   Collection Fredrik Roos
3. *Grandmother* 1984
   2 parts, 78 × 54 each
   Collection J. Jeffry Kotler
4. *Marionette, Girl* 1984
   2 parts, 72 × 48 each
   Private Collection

*5. *The Sparrows' Quarrel* 1984
   2 parts, 90 × 66 each
   Collection Robert Lehrman, Courtesy Middendorf Gallery, Washington, D.C.

## Macyn Bolt

All works are acrylic, modeling paste on styrofoam and wood; and unless otherwise indicated, courtesy the artist.

6. *Untitled* 1984
   96 × 25 × 4
7. *Untitled* 1984
   96 × 54 × 4
8. *Untitled* 1984
   93 × 20 × 4
9. *Untitled* 1984
   96 × 30 × 4
10. *Untitled* 1984
   95 × 21 × 2½
   Collection Peder Bonnier

## John Broenen

All works are oil on canvas; and courtesy the artist.

11. *Conversations with Plants* 1983
   82 × 72
12. *Night Flight* 1983
   81 × 66
13. *Still Water* 1983
   84 × 66
14. *The Squeeze Man* 1983
   76 × 76
15. *Johnny* 1984
   87 × 72

## Roger Brown

All works are oil on canvas.

*16. *The Modern Story of Life: A Civics Diatribe* 1982
   72¼ × 96
   Collection The Metropolitan Museum of Art, George A. Hearn Fund, 1983

17. *Acid Rain* 1984
   48 × 72
   Collection Mark Jackson and Ken Hodorowski
18. *Agoraphobia* 1984
   48 × 72
   Courtesy Phyllis Kind Gallery, New York and Chicago
19. *Seeking Shelter* 1984
   72 × 48
   Collection Rose and Morton Landowne
20. *The Final Arbiter* 1984
   72 × 108
   Courtesy Stefan T. Edlis/Neeson Collection

## Peter Huttinger

All works are mixed media on paper; and unless otherwise indicated, courtesy Toni Birckhead Gallery, Cincinnati, and Feature, Chicago.

21. *Love (for Jesus)*
    *Know Where Your Values Lie (for Judas)* 1983
    2 pieces, 22 × 30 each
22. *Lots* 1984
    9 pieces, 30 × 22 each
23. *Pair* 1984
    2 pieces, 30 × 22 each
24. *The (un)Related Drawings* 1984
    9 pieces, 22 × 30 each
    Courtesy Toni Birckhead Gallery, Cincinnati

## Tom Keesee

All works are oil on canvas.

25. *Adam and Eve* 1983
    36 × 50
    Collection Dr. Robert Lebow
26. *The Flood* 1983
    50 × 60
    Courtesy Patrick King Contemporary Art, Indianapolis
27. *The Professor* 1983
    43 × 33
    Collection Dr. Mary Jo Brandt
28. *The Whispering* 1983
    48 × 33
    Collection Patrick King

## Lance Kiland

All works are oil, wax on canvas.

29. *Divining Rod* 1983
    96 × 78
    Courtesy Peter Miller Gallery, Chicago
30. *Eternal Flame* 1983
    48 × 72
    Courtesy Peter Miller Gallery, Chicago
31. *New Life* 1983
    60 × 48
    Courtesy the artist
32. *Red Object Thinking* 1983
    48 × 60
    Courtesy Getler/Pall/Saper Gallery, New York
33. *Torsos* 1983
    96 × 78
    Courtesy Peter Miller Gallery, Chicago

## Robert Lostutter

All works are watercolor on paper; 1¾ × 5⅝.

34. *Violet-tailed Sylph and Crimson Topaz* 1983
    Collection Dr. and Mrs. Jorge Schneider
35. *Lovely Hummingbird and Prevosts Mango* 1984
    Collection Dr. and Mrs. Steven Valfer
36. *Goulds-jewelfront and Blue-throated Hummingbird* 1984
37. *Rivolis Hummingbird and Purple-backed Thornbill* 1984
38. *Sword-billed Hummingbird and Rufous Hummingbird* 1984
    Collection the artist, courtesy Dart Gallery, Chicago

## Jim Lutes

All works are oil on canvas.

39. *Artist in his Studio* 1982
    61 × 40½
    Courtesy James Varchmin Gallery/Lonn Frye, Chicago
40. *Jane Gets Her Way* 1982
    52 × 71
    Collection James P. Gardiner
41. *Death and the Bulldog* 1983
    60 × 84
    Courtesy Dart Gallery, Chicago
42. *Mad Cat* 1983
    42 × 48
    Courtesy Dart Gallery, Chicago
43. *Mr. Business* 1983
    42 × 53¼
    Collection Marc and Phyllis Goldish

## Kay Miller

All works are oil on canvas.

44. *Black Bear Bundle* 1984
    48 × 58
    Collection Dorothy Sahn
45. *Deep Sea Diver* 1984
    48 × 60
    Collection Dorothy Schramm
46. *Peace Walk* 1984
    52 × 72
    Courtesy the artist
47. *Scouting* 1984
    48 × 60
    Courtesy the artist
48. *Vision Quest* 1984
    49 × 60
    Courtesy the artist

## Michael Nakoneczny

All works are mixed media on masonite; and unless otherwise indicated, courtesy the artist.

49. *Crossing Wires* 1984
    27 × 36
50. *Finger Spelling* 1984
    20 × 30
51. *Native Tongue* 1984
    17 × 22
    Collection James I.W. Corcoran
52. *Quarantined* 1984
    32 × 43
53. *3 A.M.* 1984
    17 × 22

## Dennis Nechvatal

All works are courtesy Zolla/Lieberman Gallery, Chicago.

54. *Self-portrait Diptych* 1982
    oil on panel
    48 × 96
    Collection Paul A. Anderson
55. *Mary* 1983
    oil on canvas
    86 × 66
    Collection Emily and Roger Hill
56. *Youth I* 1983
    oil on canvas
    87 × 66
    Collection Walter and Dawn Clark Netsch

## Ken Nevadomi

All works are acrylic on canvas.

57. *Adam and Eve Dance with the Animals* 1983
    66 × 78
    Courtesy Osuna Gallery, Washington, D.C.
58. *Hilter in Hell* 1983
    67 × 55½
    Courtesy the artist
59. *Political Deviant with Keeper* 1983
    60 × 66
    Courtesy the artist
60. *Sky with Falling Men* 1983
    66 × 64¼
    Courtesy Osuna Gallery, Washington, D.C.

## Jim Nutt

61. *Both are Possible!!* 1982
    acrylic on canvas and wood
    19¾ × 21¾
    Collection Martin Sklar
62. *New things are a foot* 1982
    acrylic on masonite and wood
    23¼ × 21¼
    Courtesy Phyllis Kind Gallery, New York and Chicago

**63. *"Seems Simple!!"* 1982
    acrylic on canvas and wood
    22⅜ × 22⅜
    Collection Sherry and Alan Koppel

64. *Obscure delites* 1984
    acrylic on masonite and wood
    23⅛ × 21⅛
    Collection Memphis Brooks Museum of Art; Purchased by Art Today and Susan Austin, Eleanor Baer, Robert Fogelman, Allen and Minna Glenn, Wil and Sally Hergenrader, Mickey Laukhuff, Bickie McDonnell, Stella Menke, Jan Singer, Marie Thompson, Ruth Williams, and Richard and Barbara Wilson
65. *Observe the conVeNient Excuse* 1984
    acrylic on masonite and wood
    30 15/16 × 31⅜
    Collection Robert H. Bergman

## Ed Paschke

All works are oil on canvas.

66. *Bahamas* 1983
    80 × 92
    Collection Laura-Lee Woods
67. *Jupiter* 1983
    50 × 80
    Collection Daniel and Daisy Belin

*68. *La Bomba* 1983
    52 × 80
    Collection Charles B. Benenson

69. *Tropanique* 1983
    80 × 96
    Private collection
70. *Afrique* 1984
    42 × 82
    Collection Bruce and Lois Berry

## Hollis Sigler

All works are oil on canvas.

71. *Mysterious Delights of the Heart* 1983
    60 × 60
    Collection Patricia Locke

**72. *Vessi d'Ignato Amor* 1983
    48 × 60
    Collection Erwin B. and Barbara Glass

73. *Claiming a Piece of the Divine* 1984
    72 × 84
    Courtesy Barbara Gladstone Gallery, New York

74. *Desire Released* 1984
    60 × 60
    Courtesy Dart Gallery

75. *The World is Endless Desire* 1984
    60 × 60
    Collection the artist

## T.L. Solien

Unless otherwise indicated, all works are oil on canvas; 84 × 84.

76. *Voyage of the Tin Man* 1983
    Collection Steven Berkowitz

77. *The Sower* 1984
    Collection Mr. and Mrs. Robert C. Larson

78. *The Straw Ox Catches the Devil* 1984
    Collection Corrine and Leonard Lemberg

79. *Thirst/Song of the Mourning Dove* 1984
    84 × 42
    Collection Museum of Art, Rhode Island School of Design, The Albert Pilavin Collection of Twentieth Century American Art

80. *The Tree of Life* 1984
    oil, alkyd, wax on canvas
    96 × 72
    Collection First Bank Minneapolis, Courtesy Getler/Pall/Saper Gallery, New York

# BIOGRAPHIES OF THE ARTISTS

## Nicholas Africano

Born 1948, Kankakee, Illinois.

Studied Illinois State University, Normal, B.A. 1970, M.F.A. 1974.

Lives Normal, Illinois.

### Selected Individual Exhibitions

1976 Nancy Lurie Gallery, Chicago

1977 Sheldon Memorial Art Gallery, Lincoln, Nebraska
"Daddy's Old," Holly Solomon Gallery, New York
New Concepts Gallery, University of Iowa, Iowa City
"Insulin," Holly Solomon Gallery, New York
Fine Arts Center, University of Rhode Island, Kingston

1978 "The Man Who Lived in a Hat," Walker Art Center, Minneapolis

1979 "The Battered Woman," Holly Solomon Gallery, New York
Asher/Faure Gallery, Los Angeles
Galerie Farideh Cadot, Paris

1980 Holly Solomon Gallery, New York
Rotterdamse Kunststichting, Rotterdam, The Netherlands

1981 "The Girl of the Golden West," Holly Solomon Gallery, New York

1982 "Schilderigen," American Graffiti Gallery, Amsterdam
"Dr. Jekyll and Mr. Hyde: The Crisis Between Knowledge and Faith," Holly Solomon Gallery, New York

1983 "Nicholas Africano: Paintings 1976–1983," North Carolina Museum of Art, Raleigh
"Nicholas Africano: Petrouchka Paintings and Other New Work," Middendorf Gallery, Washington, D.C.

1984 Holly Solomon Gallery, New York

### Selected Group Exhibitions

1976 "Illinois Artists 76," Illinois State University, Normal

1977 "1977 Biennial Exhibition," Whitney Museum of American Art, New York
"American Painting '75, '76, '77," Sarah Lawrence College Gallery, Bronxville, New York
"A Painting Show," Institute for Art and Urban Resources, P.S. 1, Long Island City, Queens, New York
"The 1977 Annual Exhibition," San Francisco Art Institute

1978 "Narration," Institute of Contemporary Art, Boston
"The Sense of Self," Neuberger Museum, Purchase, New York
"Painting and Sculpture Today 1978," Indianapolis Museum of Art

1979 "New Image Painting," Whitney Museum of American Art, New York
"Words and Images," Philadelphia College of Art
"American Portraits of the 60's and 70's," Aspen Center for the Visual Arts

1980 "First Person Singular: Recent Self-Portraiture," Pratt Institute Gallery, Brooklyn, New York
"American Painting Show," XIII Olympic Winter Games, Lake Placid, New York
"Painting in Relief," Whitney Museum of American Art, Downtown Branch, New York
"Les Nouveaux Fauves—Die Neuen Wilden," Neue Galerie/Sammlung Ludwig, Aachen, West Germany
"The Pluralist Decade," United States Pavilion, Venice Biennale
"Chicago/Chicago," Contemporary Arts Center, Cincinnati, Ohio
"Tableau, An American Selection," Middendorf/Lane Gallery, Washington, D.C.

1981 "Contemporary Drawings in Search of an Image," University Art Museum, University of California, Santa Barbara
"Aspects of Post-Modernism: Decorative and Narrative Art," The Squibb Gallery, Princeton, New Jersey

1982 "Painting and Sculpture Today 1982," Indianapolis Museum of Art
"New York Now," Kestner-Gesellschaft, Hannover, West Germany

1983 "New Image—Pattern and Decoration," Kalamazoo Institute of Arts, Kalamazoo, Michigan
"Made in America: 200 Years of Drawing," The Minneapolis Institute of Arts
"Language, Drama, Source, & Vision," The New Museum of Contemporary Art, New York
"Back to the U.S.A.," Kunstmuseum, Luzern

1984 "An International Survey of Recent Painting and Sculpture," The Museum of Modern Art, New York
"Via New York," Musée d'Art Contemporain, Montreal
"The Human Condition," Biennial III, San Francisco Museum of Modern Art

## Macyn Bolt

Born 1954, Fort Knox, Kentucky.

Studied Grand Valley State Colleges, William James College, Allendale, Michigan; Calvin College, Grand Rapids, Michigan, B.F.A. 1979; Syracuse University, New York, M.F.A. 1981.

Lives Grand Rapids, Michigan.

### Selected Individual Exhibitions

1980 Fairbanks Gallery, Syracuse, New York
1982 Ferris State College, Big Rapids, Michigan
Race Street Gallery, Grand Rapids, Michigan
1983 "Power and Coercion," Race Street Gallery, Grand Rapids, Michigan
1984 University Art Gallery, Central Michigan University, Mount Pleasant

### Selected Group Exhibitions

1979 "42nd Annual Exhibition of Central New York," Munson-Williams-Proctor Museum, Utica, New York
1980 "The Syracuse Show 1980," Everson Museum of Art, Syracuse, New York
1981 "Chautauqua National Exhibition of American Art," Chautauqua Institution, Chautauqua, New York
1982 "Nuclear Arms, Strategic Weapons: The Artist's Vision," University Art Gallery, Central Michigan University, Mount Pleasant
1983 Contemporary Art Workshop, Chicago
1984 "Totem," Bonnier Gallery, New York

## John Broenen

Born 1959, Milwaukee, Wisconsin.

Studied University of Wisconsin, Milwaukee, B.F.A. 1981

Lives Milwaukee, Wisconsin.

### Selected Individual Exhibitions

1983 Two Illinois Center, Chicago
1984 University of Wisconsin, Marshfield

### Selected Group Exhibitions

1982 "1982 Wisconsin Biennial," Madison Art Center, Madison, Wisconsin
1983 "26th Annual Beloit and Vicinity Exhibition," Wright Art Center, Beloit College, Beloit, Wisconsin
"Emerging Imagists," Milwaukee Art Museum
"Wisconsin Focus," Milwaukee Art Museum
1984 "Wisconsin Directions 4," Milwaukee Art Museum

## Roger Brown

Born 1941, Hamilton, Alabama.

Studied School of The Art Institute of Chicago, B.F.A. 1968, M.F.A. 1970.

Lives Chicago, Illinois.

### Selected Individual Exhibitions

1979 Phyllis Kind Gallery, Chicago and New York
1980 "Roger Brown," Montgomery Museum of Fine Art, Montgomery, Alabama
"Currents," The St. Louis Art Museum
1981 The Mayor Gallery, London
1982 Phyllis Kind Gallery, Chicago and New York
1983 Asher/Faure Gallery, Los Angeles
1984 Phyllis Kind Gallery, New York

### Selected Group Exhibitions

1969 "Spirit of the Comics," Institute of Contemporary Art, University of Pennsylvania, Philadelphia
"Don Baum Sez 'Chicago Needs Famous Artists,' " Museum of Contemporary Art, Chicago
1970 "Surplus Slop from the Windy City," San Francisco Art Institute
"Prints by Seven," Whitney Museum of American Art, New York
1971 "73rd Exhibition by Artists of Chicago and Vicinity," The Art Institute of Chicago
1972 "Chicago Imagist Art," Museum of Contemporary Art, Chicago
1974 "1974 Biennial Exhibition," Whitney Museum of American Art, New York
"75th Exhibition by Artists of Chicago and Vicinity," The Art Institute of Chicago
1976 "The Chicago Connection," E.B. Crocker Art Gallery, Sacramento, California
1977 "View of a Decade," Museum of Contemporary Art, Chicago
"76th Exhibition by Artists of Chicago and Vicinity," The Art Institute of Chicago
1978 "American Painting of the 1970's," Albright-Knox Art Gallery, Buffalo, New York
"Eleven Chicago Painters," University Gallery, Florida State University, Tallahassee

1979 "1979 Biennial Exhibition," Whitney Museum of American Art, New York

"Art, Inc.: American Painting from Corporate Collections," Montgomery Museum of Fine Art, Montgomery, Alabama

"The Nineteen Seventies: New American Painting," traveling exhibition to Eastern Europe organized by the International Communications Agency

1980 "Who Chicago? An Exhibition of Contemporary Imagists," Sunderland Arts Centre, England

"Six Artists From Chicago," The Mayor Gallery, London

"Image Into Pattern," Institute for Art and Urban Resources, P.S. 1, Long Island City, Queens, New York

"The Figurative Tradition and the Whitney Museum of American Art," Whitney Museum of American Art, New York

"Some Recent Art from Chicago," The Ackland Art Museum, University of North Carolina, Chapel Hill

1981 "Contemporary Artists," The Cleveland Museum of Art

"American Landscape: Recent Developments," Whitney Museum of American Art, New York

"Religion Into Art," Pratt Manhattan Center Gallery, New York

1982 "Recent Directions," Milwaukee Art Museum

"The Atomic Salon," Ronald Feldman Gallery, New York

"Painting and Sculpture Today 1982," Indianapolis Museum of Art

"Selections from the Dennis Adrian Collection," Museum of Contemporary Art, Chicago

"From Chicago," The Pace Gallery

1983 "New American Painting: A Tribute to James and Mari Michener," Archer M. Huntington Art Gallery, University of Texas, Austin

"The End of the World: Contemporary Visions of the Apocalypse," The New Museum of Contemporary Art, New York

"Brave New Works: Recent American Painting and Drawing," Museum of Fine Arts, Boston

"Ten New Narrative Paintings," The Metropolitan Museum of Art, New York

"Brown, Nutt and Paschke," Galerie Rudolf Zwirner, Cologne, West Germany

"Contemporary Landscape Painting," Freedman Gallery, Albright College, Reading, Pennsylvania

1984 "Contemporary Focus: 1974 through 1984," Hirshhorn Museum and Sculpture Garden, Washington, D.C.

"Paradise Lost, Paradise Regained: American Visions of the New Decade," United States Pavilion, Venice Biennale

"An International Survey of Recent Painting and Sculpture," The Museum of Modern Art, New York

"Ten Years of Collecting at the MCA," Museum of Contemporary Art, Chicago

"Auto and Culture," The Museum of Contemporary Art, Los Angeles

"Joseph Yoakum: His Influence on Contemporary Art and Artists," Carl Hammer Gallery, Chicago

## Peter Huttinger

Born 1953, West Palm Beach, Florida.

Lives Cincinnati, Ohio.

Exhibitions are not included at the artist's request.

## Tom Keesee

Born 1954, Crawfordsville, Indiana.

Studied Herron School of Art, Indianapolis, Indiana, B.F.A. 1977; Miami University, Oxford, Ohio, M.F.A. 1981.

Lives Indianapolis, Indiana.

### Selected Individual Exhibitions

1981 Hiestand Gallery, Miami University, Oxford, Ohio

### Selected Group Exhibitions

1982 "Small Works," 80 Washington Square East Gallery, New York University, New York

"Works on Walls, Exhibition 280," Huntington Galleries, Huntington, West Virginia

"Whitewater Valley Annual Art Exhibition," Indiana University East, Richmond

Art League Regional, Churchman-Fehsenfeld Gallery, Indianapolis Art League

Patrick King Contemporary Art, Indianapolis

1983 "69th Indiana Artists Exhibition," Indianapolis Museum of Art

"The Building Show," Churchman-Fehsenfeld Gallery, Indianapolis Art League

"American Artists/Indianapolis," Patrick King Contemporary Art, Indianapolis

## Lance Kiland

Born 1947, Fargo, North Dakota.

Studied Moorhead State University, Moorhead, Minnesota, B.A. 1969; Southern Illinois University, Carbondale, M.F.A. 1971.

Lives Minneapolis, Minnesota.

### Selected Individual Exhibitions

1977 St. John's University, Collegeville, Minnesota
1981 Groveland Gallery, Minneapolis
1982 Hamline University, St. Paul
Peter Miller Gallery, Chicago
1983 Thomson Gallery, Minneapolis
Getler/Pall/Saper Gallery, New York
1984 St. Cloud State University, St. Cloud, Minnesota
Peter Miller Gallery, Chicago

### Selected Group Exhibitions

1974 "Manisphere," Winnipeg Art Gallery, Winnipeg, Manitoba
1975 J. Hunt Gallery, Minneapolis
"Friends Gallery Group Show," The Minneapolis Institute of Arts, Minneapolis
1976 Rochester Art Center, Rochester, Minnesota
1977 "Friends Gallery Group Show," The Minneapolis Institute of Arts
1978 "Drawing and Small Sculpture Show," Art Gallery, Ball State University, Muncie, Indiana
1979 "Waterworks," Groveland Gallery, Minneapolis
1981 "Art and the Law," Minnesota Museum of Art, St. Paul
Glen Hanson Gallery, Minneapolis
1982 Peter Miller Gallery, Chicago
"The Bewildered Image," The Minneapolis Institute of Arts
Ericson Gallery, New York
1983 "Batten Down the Hatches," Peter Miller Gallery, Chicago
Getler/Pall/Saper Gallery, New York
"1983 Biennial Exhibition," Whitney Museum of American Art, New York
1984 "Rooted in North Dakota," North Dakota Museum of Art, Grand Forks

## Robert Lostutter

Born 1939, Emporia, Kansas.

Studied School of The Art Institute of Chicago.

Lives Chicago, Illinois.

### Selected Individual Exhibitions

1972 DeMarco Gallery, Edinburgh, Scotland
1975 Deson-Zaks Gallery, Chicago
1976 Dart Gallery, Chicago
1978 "Recent Work," Dart Gallery, Chicago
1980 "Works on Paper," Dart Gallery, Chicago
1981 "New Paintings," Monique Knowlton Gallery, New York
1984 "Works on Paper," Dart Gallery, Chicago
"Robert Lostutter: The Watercolors," The Renaissance Society at the University of Chicago

### Selected Group Exhibitions

1972 "After Surrealism: Metaphor and Similes," John and Mabel Ringling Museum of Art, Sarasota, Florida
"Painting and Sculpture Today 1972," Indianapolis Museum of Art
1973 "74th Exhibition by Artists of Chicago and Vicinity," The Art Institute of Chicago
1974 "Nineteenth National Print Exhibition," The Brooklyn Museum
1975 "North, East, West, South and Middle: Drawings," Moore College of Art, Philadelphia
1976 "Visions: Distinguished Alumni 1945 to Present," School of The Art Institute of Chicago
"The Chicago Connection," E.B. Crocker Art Gallery, Sacramento, California
1977 "Masterpieces of Recent Chicago Art," Chicago Public Library Cultural Center
"The 1977 Annual Exhibition," San Francisco Art Institute
1978 "Chicago Collects Chicago," Swen Parson Gallery, Northern Illinois University, DeKalb
"Chicago: Self-Portraits," Nancy Lurie Gallery, Chicago
"Works on Paper," The Art Institute of Chicago
1979 "Artists Paint Artists," Evanston Art Center, Evanston, Illinois
1980 "Masters of American Watercolor," Joslyn Art Museum, Omaha, Nebraska
"Chicago and Vicinity: Prizewinners Revisited (Part II)," The Art Institute of Chicago
"Touch Me," N.A.M.E. Gallery, Chicago
1981 "Drawing from Chicago," Sheldon Memorial Art Gallery, University of Nebraska, Lincoln
1982 "Drawing New Directions," Summit Art Center, Summit, New Jersey
"Hot Chicago," Douglas Drake Gallery, Kansas City, Missouri

1983 "Contemporary Images: Watercolor, 1983," Allen Priebe Gallery, University of Wisconsin, Oshkosh
"Chicago: Some Other Traditions," Madison Art Center, Madison, Wisconsin

## Jim Lutes

Born 1955, Fort Lewis, Washington.

Studied Washington State University, Pullman, Washington, B.A. 1978; School of The Art Institute of Chicago, M.F.A. 1982.

Lives Chicago, Illinois.

### Selected Group Exhibitions

1978 "Off the Wall," Gallery II, Pullman, Washington

1983 "Jim Lutes/Jin Soo Kim," Randolph Street Gallery, Chicago
"Emerging," The Renaissance Society at the University of Chicago
"Fantastic Visions," Hyde Park Art Center, Chicago

1984 "80th Exhibition by Artists of Chicago and Vicinity," The Art Institute of Chicago
"New Talent," Hal Bromm Gallery, New York
"Chicago 1984: Artists to Watch," Dart Gallery, Chicago

## Kay Miller

Born 1946, Houston, Texas.

Studied University of Houston, B.S. 1970; University of Texas, Austin, B.F.A. 1975, M.F.A. 1978; Naropa Institute, Boulder, Colorado, 1978.

Lives Iowa City, Iowa.

### Selected Individual Exhibitions

1978 "Free Art/Free Love/Free Money," Archer M. Huntington Art Gallery, University of Texas, Austin

1983 Formal Gallery, West Texas University, Canyon

1984 "Current Connector," Museum of Art, University of Iowa, Iowa City

### Selected Group Exhibitions

1976 "Texas Women," Armadillo World Headquarters, Austin, Texas

1977 "New Age Painters," Pecan Gallery, Austin, Texas
"15 Waves," Trinity Gallery, Austin, Texas

1979 "Women-in-Sight," Soughtery Cultural Arts Center, Austin, Texas

1981 "Plains Primitive," Gallery 72, Omaha, Nebraska

1983 "Discovery," Minnesota Museum of Art, St. Paul
"Contemporary Native American Art," Gardiner Art Gallery, Oklahoma State University, Stillwater

1984 "New Work: New York/Outside New York," The New Museum of Contemporary Art, New York
"New Symbolists," Sioux City Art Center, Sioux City, Iowa
"Emerging Artists," Minnesota Museum of Art, St. Paul

## Michael Nakoneczny

Born 1952, Detroit, Michigan.

Studied Cleveland Engineering Institute, Cleveland, Ohio, A.D. 1972; Kent State University, Kent, Ohio, 1973–76; Cleveland State University, Cleveland, Ohio, B.A. 1979; University of Cincinnati, Cincinnati, Ohio, M.F.A. 1981.

Lives Cincinnati, Ohio.

### Selected Individual Exhibitions

1981 Tangeman Fine Arts Gallery, University of Cincinnati, Cincinnati, Ohio
Piedmont Art Gallery, Augusta, Kentucky

1982 Carnegie Art Center, Covington, Kentucky

### Selected Group Exhibitions

1980 "33rd Annual Mid-States Art Exhibit," Evansville Museum of Arts and Sciences, Evansville, Indiana

1981 "6 Artists Ohio/6 Artists Indiana," Cranbrook Academy of Art Museum, Bloomfield Hills, Michigan

1982 "Six Artists," Toni Birckhead Gallery, Cincinnati, Ohio
"Figure '82," Contemporary Arts Center, Cincinnati, Ohio

1983 Carnegie Art Center, Covington, Kentucky
"Four Artists," C.A.G.E. Gallery, Cincinnati, Ohio
"Figuratively Speaking: 8 Ohio Figurative Artists," Art Gallery, Cleveland State University, Cleveland, Ohio

1984 "Drawn to Cincinnati," Contemporary Arts Center, Cincinnati, Ohio
"Artists' Spaces Collaborate," Spaces, Cleveland, Ohio

## Dennis Nechvatal

Born 1948, Dodgeville, Wisconsin.

Studied Loras College, Dubuque, Iowa, 1966-67; Stout State University, Menomonie, Wisconsin, B.S., B.A. 1971; Indiana University, Bloomington, M.F.A. 1974.

Lives Madison, Wisconsin.

Selected Individual Exhibitions

1977 University of Colorado, Colorado Springs
 Water Street Art Center, Milwaukee
1979 Triton Museum of Art, Santa Clara, California
 Water Street Art Center, Milwaukee
1980 Zolla/Lieberman Gallery, Chicago
1981 Center for the Visual Arts Gallery, Illinois State University, Normal
1982 Zolla/Lieberman Gallery, Chicago
 "Dennis Nechvatal: Paintings and Drawings," Madison Art Center, Madison, Wisconsin
1983 "Dennis Nechvatal: Images for a New Age," Herron Gallery, Herron School of Art of Indiana University, Indianapolis
1984 Siegel Contemporary Art, New York

Selected Group Exhibitions

1979 "New Talent—New Visions," Zolla/Lieberman Gallery, Chicago
1981 "Inside/Out: Self Beyond Likeness," Newport Harbor Art Museum, Newport Beach, California
 "Fifty Works of Art that Shouldn't Leave Madison," Madison Art Center, Madison, Wisconsin
1982 "Painting and Sculpture Today 1982," Indianapolis Museum of Art
 "New Faces—Old Friends," Madison Art Center, Madison, Wisconsin
1983 "Contemporary Images: Watercolor 1983," Allen Priebe Gallery, University of Wisconsin, Oshkosh
 "Emerging Imagists," Milwaukee Art Museum
 "Living with Art, Two: The Collection of Walter and Dawn Clark Netsch," Art Museum, Miami University, Oxford, Ohio
1984 "Chicago: Emerging Visions," Paine Art Center, Oshkosh, Wisconsin
 "Painting and Sculpture Today 1984," Indianapolis Museum of Art
 "Lines of Beauty: A Drawing Exhibition," Zolla/Lieberman Gallery, Chicago
 "Wisconsin Directions 4," Milwaukee Art Museum

## Ken Nevadomi

Born 1939, Cleveland, Ohio.

Studied Cooper School of Art, Cleveland, Ohio, A.D. 1967; Columbus College of Art and Design, Columbus, Ohio, B.F.A. 1972; Kent State University, Kent, Ohio, M.F.A. 1975.

Lives Lakewood, Ohio.

Selected Individual Exhibitions

1975 Akron Art Museum, Akron, Ohio
1977 Art Galleries, Kent State University, Kent, Ohio
 Seigfred Gallery, Ohio University, Athens
1978 Tangeman Fine Arts Center, University of Cincinnati, Cincinnati, Ohio
1980 Art Gallery, Cleveland State University, Cleveland, Ohio
1983 "Neon & Noire," Spaces, Cleveland, Ohio

Selected Group Exhibitions

1977 Linden Gallery, Cleveland, Ohio
1978 "Rips in Reality," Akron Art Museum, Akron, Ohio
 "Cleveland Exchange," Art Gallery, Cleveland State University, Cleveland, Ohio
1979 "Surrealism Now," Spaces, Cleveland, Ohio
 "The 1979 May Show," The Cleveland Museum of Art
 "Four Figurative Painters," The Canton Art Institute, Canton, Ohio
 Jane Vorhees Zimmerli Art Museum, Rutgers University, New Brunswick, New Jersey
1980 "Outside New York: The State of Ohio," The New Museum of Contemporary Art, New York
1981 "Rutger's National Drawing Show," Stedman Art Gallery, Rutgers University, Camden, New Jersey
1982 Bonfoey's on the Square, Cleveland, Ohio
1983 "The 47th National Annual Butler Show," The Butler Institute of American Art, Youngstown, Ohio

## Jim Nutt

Born 1938, Pittsfield, Massachusetts.

Studied School of The Art Institute of Chicago, B.F.A. 1965.

Lives Wilmette, Illinois.

Selected Individual Exhibitions

1975 Portland Center for the Visual Arts, Portland, Oregon
 San Francisco Art Institute
1977 Phyllis Kind Gallery, New York
1979 Phyllis Kind Gallery, Chicago
1980 Rotterdamse Kunststichting, Rotterdam, The Netherlands
1982 Phyllis Kind Gallery, Chicago
1983 The Mayor Gallery, London
1984 Phyllis Kind Gallery, New York

#### Selected Group Exhibitions

1967 "The Hairy Who," Hyde Park Art Center, Chicago

1969 "Spirit of the Comics," Institute of Contemporary Art, University of Pennsylvania, Philadelphia

"Don Baum Sez 'Chicago Needs Famous Artists,' " Museum of Contemporary Art, Chicago

"Da Hairy Who," DuPont Center, The Corcoran Gallery of Art, Washington, D.C.

"Human Concern/Personal Torment," Whitney Museum of American Art, New York

1970 "Surplus Slop from the Windy City," San Francisco Art Institute

1972 "Chicago Imagist Art," Museum of Contemporary Art, Chicago

"What They're Up To in Chicago," National Gallery of Canada, Ottawa

1973 "Made in Chicago," XII Bienal de Sao Paolo, Brazil

1975 "Art Now," Artrend Foundation, The John F. Kennedy Center for the Performing Arts, Washington, D.C.

1976 "72nd American Exhibition," The Art Institute of Chicago

1977 "View of a Decade," Museum of Contemporary Art, Chicago

"1977 Biennial Exhibition," Whitney Museum of American Art, New York

1978 "Contemporary Chicago Painters," Gallery of Art, University of Northern Iowa, Cedar Rapids

1979 "The Nineteen Seventies: New American Painting," traveling exhibition to Eastern Europe organized by the International Communications Agency

1980 "Six Artists from Chicago," The Mayor Gallery, London

"American Figure Painting 1950–1980," The Chrysler Museum, Norfolk, Virginia

"American Drawings in Black and White," The Brooklyn Museum

"Some Recent Art from Chicago," The Ackland Art Museum, University of North Carolina, Chapel Hill

"Who Chicago? An Exhibition of Contemporary Imagists," Sunderland Arts Centre, England

1981 "American Painting 1930–1980," Haus der Kunst, Munich, West Germany

"New Dimensions in Drawing 1950–1980," The Aldrich Museum of Contemporary Art, Ridgefield, Connecticut

1982 "Dialect≠Dialectic: A Group Show of Artists with Complex Individual Vocabularies," Phyllis Kind Gallery, New York and Chicago

"The Erotic Impulse," Roger Litz Gallery, New York

"Focus on the Figure: Twenty Years," Whitney Museum of American Art, New York

"Chicago on Paper," Ray Hughes Gallery, Brisbane, Australia

"Recent Directions," Milwaukee Art Museum

"Selections from the Dennis Adrian Collection," Museum of Contemporary Art, Chicago

1983 "The Comic Show," Whitney Museum of American Art, Federal Hall, New York

"Gladys Nilsson, Jim Nutt, Ed Paschke, Suellen Rocca, Karl Wirsum," Galerie Bonnier, Geneva, Switzerland

"The Last Laugh," Southern Ohio Museum and Cultural Center, Portsmouth, Ohio

"Intoxication," Monique Knowlton Gallery, New York

"Brown, Nutt and Paschke," Galerie Rudolf Zwirner, Cologne, West Germany

"Contemporary Chicago Imagists," Illinois Wesleyan University, Bloomington

1984 "Contemporary Focus: 1974 through 1984," Hirshhorn Museum and Sculpture Garden, Washington, D.C.

"Strange," Henry Art Gallery, University of Washington, Seattle

"Ten Years of Collecting at the MCA," Museum of Contemporary Art, Chicago

"Joseph Yoakum: His Influence on Contemporary Art and Artists," Carl Hammer Gallery, Chicago

"Chicago Cross Section," Seigfred Gallery, Ohio University, Athens

### Ed Paschke

Born 1939, Chicago, Illinois.

Studied School of The Art Institute of Chicago, B.F.A. 1961, M.F.A. 1970.

Lives Chicago, Illinois.

#### Selected Individual Exhibitions

1975 Deson-Zaks Gallery, Chicago

Pyramid Gallery, Washington, D.C.

1976 Marion Locks Gallery, Philadelphia

Galerie Darthea Speyer, Paris

1977 Phyllis Kind Gallery, Chicago

1978 Galerie Darthea Speyer, Paris

Phyllis Kind Gallery, New York

1980 Phyllis Kind Gallery, New York

1982 "Ed Paschke: Selected Works 1967–1981," The Renaissance Society at the University of Chicago

Phyllis Kind Gallery, New York

1983 "New Paintings 1983," Hewlett Gallery, Carnegie Mellon University, Pittsburgh

Galerie Darthea Speyer, Paris

1984 Galerie Bonnier, Geneva, Switzerland

Fuller Goldeen Gallery, San Francisco

Phyllis Kind Gallery, New York

Selected Group Exhibitions

1969 "Spirit of the Comics," Institute of Contemporary Art, University of Pennsylvania, Philadelphia

"Don Baum Sez 'Chicago Needs Famous Artists,' " Museum of Contemporary Art, Chicago

"Human Concern/Personal Torment," Whitney Museum of American Art, New York

1970 "Surplus Slop from the Windy City," San Francisco Art Institute

1972 "Chicago Imagist Art," Museum of Contemporary Art, Chicago

"What They're Up To in Chicago," National Gallery of Canada, Ottawa

1973 "74th Exhibition by Artists of Chicago and Vicinity," The Art Institute of Chicago

"1973 Biennial Exhibition," Whitney Museum of American Art, New York

"Made in Chicago," XII Bienal de Sao Paolo, Brazil

1976 "The Chicago Connection," E.B. Crocker Art Gallery, Sacramento, California

1977 "View of a Decade," Museum of Contemporary Art, Chicago

1978 "Eleven Chicago Painters," University Gallery, Florida State University, Tallahassee

1979 "American Portraits of the 60's and 70's," Aspen Center for the Visual Arts

1980 "Some Recent Art from Chicago," The Ackland Art Museum, University of North Carolina, Chapel Hill

"Six Artists from Chicago," The Mayor Gallery, London

"Who Chicago? An Exhibition of Contemporary Imagists," Sunderland Arts Centre, England

1981 "American Painting 1930–1980," Haus der Kunst, Munich, West Germany

"1981 Biennial Exhibition," Whitney Museum of American Art, New York

"Contemporary Artists," The Cleveland Museum of Art

1982 "From Chicago," The Pace Gallery, New York

"Focus on the Figure: Twenty Years," Whitney Museum of American Art, New York

"Recent Directions," Milwaukee Art Museum

"Painting and Sculpture Today 1982," Indianapolis Museum of Art

"Selections from the Dennis Adrian Collection," Museum of Contemporary Art, Chicago

"Chicago Imagists," Kansas City Art Institute, Kansas City, Missouri

1983 "New American Painting: A Tribute to James and Mari Michener," Archer M. Huntington Art Gallery, University of Texas, Austin

"Painting and Sculpture by Candidates for Art Awards," American Academy of Arts and Letters, New York

"Gladys Nilsson, Jim Nutt, Ed Paschke, Suellen Rocca, Karl Wirsum," Galerie Bonnier, Geneva, Switzerland

"The T.V. Show," Bard College, Annandale-on-Hudson, New York

"200 Years of American Painting from Private Chicago Collections," Terra Museum of American Art, Evanston, Illinois

"Brown, Nutt and Paschke," Rudolf Zwirner Gallery, Cologne, West Germany

"What Artists Have to Say about Nuclear War," Nexus Gallery, Atlanta

"Contemporary Chicago Imagists," Illinois Wesleyan University, Bloomington

1984 "Contemporary Focus: 1974 through 1984," Hirshhorn Museum and Sculpture Garden, Washington, D.C.

"An International Survey of Recent Painting and Sculpture," The Museum of Modern Art, New York

"Ten Years of Collecting at the MCA," Museum of Contemporary Art, Chicago

"Chicago Cross Section," Seigfred Gallery, Ohio University, Athens

"Artists Call Against U.S. Intervention in Central America and the Caribbean," Rhona Hoffman Gallery, Chicago

"American Drawings 1983 from A to Z," Sutton Gallery, New York

"Alternative Spaces: A History in Chicago," Museum of Contemporary Art, Chicago

"50 Artists/50 States," Fuller Goldeen Gallery, San Francisco

## Hollis Sigler

Born 1948, Gary, Indiana.

Studied Moore College of Art, Philadelphia, B.F.A. 1970; School of The Art Institute of Chicago, M.F.A. 1973.

Lives Prairie View, Illinois.

Selected Individual Exhibitions

1977 Nancy Lurie Gallery, Chicago
1979 Barbara Gladstone Gallery, New York
Fine Arts Center, University of Rhode Island, Kingston
Nancy Lurie Gallery, Chicago
1980 Barbara Gladstone Gallery, New York
Nancy Lurie Gallery, Chicago
1981 "Poisoned," Barbara Gladstone Gallery, New York
Okun-Thomas Gallery, St. Louis, Missouri
"Incantations," Nancy Lurie Gallery, Chicago
1982 "A Journey to Somewhere from Nowhere," Barbara Gladstone Gallery, New York
Dart Gallery, Chicago
1983 Barbara Gladstone Gallery, New York

Selected Group Exhibitions

1973 "74th Exhibition by Artists of Chicago and Vicinity," The Art Institute of Chicago
1978 "Works on Paper, 77th Exhibition by Artists of Chicago and Vicinity," The Art Institute of Chicago
"Lineup," Drawing Center, New York
1979 "Portraits," Aspen Center for the Visual Arts
"Chicago Alternatives," Herron Gallery, Herron School of Art of Indiana University, Indianapolis
1980 "78th Exhibition by Artists of Chicago and Vicinity," The Art Institute of Chicago
"Interiors," Barbara Gladstone Gallery, New York
1981 "For Love and Money," Pratt Manhattan Center Gallery, New York
"Summer Pleasures," Barbara Gladstone Gallery, New York
"1981 Biennial Exhibition," Whitney Museum of American Art, New York
"Seven Artists," Museum of Contemporary Art, Chicago
"Narratives," Kathryn Markel Gallery, New York
"Fifty Works of Art That Shouldn't Leave Madison," Madison Art Center, Madison, Wisconsin
1982 "Currents: The New Mannerism," Jacksonville Art Museum, Jacksonville, Florida
"New Drawing in America: Part I," Drawing Center, New York
"The Anxious Edge," Walker Art Center, Minneapolis
"Painting and Sculpture Today 1982," Indianapolis Museum of Art
"Stroke/Line/Figure," Gimpel Fils, London
1983 "Back to the U.S.A.," Kunstmuseum, Luzern
"Sky Art: Paintings in the Air," Art and Culture Center of Hollywood, Hollywood, Florida
"Looking at Women," Artemisia Gallery, Chicago
"Personification," Thompson Gallery, Massachusetts College of Art, Boston
1984 "Visions of Childhood: A Contemporary Iconography," Whitney Museum of American Art, Downtown Branch, New York
"80th Exhibition by Artists of Chicago and Vicinity," The Art Institute of Chicago
"American Women Artists/Part II: Younger Generation," Sidney Janis Gallery, New York

## T.L. Solien

Born 1949, Fargo, North Dakota.

Studied Moorhead State University, Moorhead, Minnesota, B.A. 1973; University of Nebraska, Lincoln, M.F.A. 1977.

Lives Pelican Rapids, Minnesota.

Selected Individual Exhibitions

1979 Glen Hanson Gallery, Minneapolis
1980 The Fort Worth Museum of Art, Fort Worth, Texas
1983 Getler/Pall Gallery, New York
"Les Pierres du Minnesota," American Center, Paris
vanStraaten Gallery, Chicago
1984 Getler/Pall/Saper Gallery, New York
Cantor/Lemberg Gallery, Birmingham, Michigan

Selected Group Exhibitions

1977 "Nebraska Drawings," Syracuse University, Syracuse, New York
1980 "Prints and Multiples," Glen Hanson Gallery, Minneapolis
1981 "Minneapolis II," Dayton's Gallery 12, Minneapolis
1982 "The Bewildered Image," The Minneapolis Institute of Arts
1983 "1983 Biennial Exhibition," Whitney Museum of American Art, New York
"The American Artist as Printmaker," The Brooklyn Museum
1984 "Images and Impressions," Walker Art Center, Minneapolis
"Here and Now," Greenville County Museum of Art, Greenville, South Carolina
"Contemporary American Art," Columbus Museum of Arts and Sciences, Columbus, Georgia
"Rooted in North Dakota," North Dakota Museum of Art, Grand Forks
"Images and Impressions: Painters Who Print," Walker Art Center, Minneapolis

PHOTOGRAPHY CREDITS

| ARTIST | PHOTOGRAPHER |
|---|---|
| Nicholas Africano | Joel Breger |
| Macyn Bolt | Craig Vander Lende |
| John Broenen | Dedra M. Walls |
| Roger Brown | William H. Bengtson |
| Peter Huttinger | Tony Walsh |
| Tom Keesee | Robert Wallace |
| Lance Kiland | Jerry Mathiason |
| Robert Lostutter | Michael Tropea |
| Jim Lutes | Michael Tropea |
| Kay Miller | Randall Tosh |
| Michael Nakoneczny | Jay Bachemin |
| Dennis Nechvatal | John Bolton |
| Ken Nevadomi | Joel Breger |
| Jim Nutt | William H. Bengtson |
| Ed Paschke | William H. Bengtson |
| Hollis Sigler | Michael Tropea |
| T.L. Solien | R.H. Hensleigh |